FEMALE MONOLOGUES from PUBLISHED PLAYS

102 MONOLOGUES FOR TEENS & ADULTS

Edited by Debra Fendrich

MERIWETHER PUBLISHING
A division of Pioneer Drama Service, Inc.
Denver, Colorado

Meriwether Publishing
A division of Pioneer Drama Service, Inc.
PO Box 4267
Englewood, CO 80155

www.pioneerdrama.com

Editor: Debra Fendrich
Assistant Editor: Brian D. Taylor
Cover design: Mel Nethery
Text design: Lori Conary

© Copyright 2022 Meriwether Publishing

Printed in the United States of America
First Edition

ISBN: 978-1-56608-271-6

Library of Congress Control Number: 2022937193

1   2   3   22   23   24

Contents

* The letter in parentheses indicates the overall tone of the monologue: (C) comedic, (S) seriocomic, (D) dramatic. See Appendix A for a list of monologues by tone.

Introduction

Finding the "right" monologue is usually a bit of a chore. It's rarely easy or obvious which one to select for any given project. That's typically because monologues are used for a wide variety of purposes. You might be seeking a monologue for an audition. Or maybe you are looking for a piece for competition. Perhaps you need to find a suitable monologue for an acting exercise in a theatre class.

And there are so many different types of monologues from which to choose! Some are simply an interesting narrative. Others capture a moment of raw emotion. Some call for an interesting accent or stage action that can showcase a certain skill set or strength. Of course, some are dramatic, some are comedic, and some are somewhere in between or have elements of both. Ideally, they have a beginning, middle, and end, but not always.

On top of all this, there are the vexing questions about the audience for your monologue. "What piece is most likely to sway the director?" "Should I choose something more technically challenging to impress the adjudicator or something more deep and thoughtful?" "Should I select something that will highlight my strengths?" "Will I shine the most if I perform the monologue that I like best?"

Our best advice for you is that the end determines the means in the pursuit of the "right" monologue. You almost always need to begin at the end and try to work backwards. Consider what you think the director wants or what the producers are casting for, then go find that. "But what about this...? And that...?" You're often left trying to read the mind of a stranger, leaving you to feel that the perfect monologue is impossible to find!

With this book of monologues, our aim is to minimize this frustration. We have carefully crafted it to include as many different types of monologues as possible. Our goal is to include a strong and varied collection of monologues that addresses a broad spectrum of needs so that everyone who uses this book can find the "right" monologue every time they need one.

To this end, you will find the appendices at the back of the book to be invaluable tools. A quick scan through these pages will help you quickly and easily identify the monologues that portray a character of a certain age or that are from a specific time period. Most books focus on characters of a narrow age range, almost always in the present day. Not this one! Here you will find characters as young as their early teens and as old as their 60s. Likewise, you'll find plenty of monologues that take place now, but almost as many that take place in a bygone era, whether it be decades or centuries ago. And unlike other monologue books, this collection also offers you a wide variety of running times, with some selections as short as 45 seconds and others five minutes or longer.

The table of contents and the appendices also indicate the overall tone of the monologue, whether it be comedic (C), dramatic (D), or seriocomic (S), meaning it either has elements of both or is neither remarkably funny nor delving deep into strong emotion. And you might be surprised. The tone of a particular monologue does not always align with the overall tone of the play it comes from. Rather, it's about that one character at that particular moment in the play.

No doubt, capturing the character is the most vital aspect of performing a monologue—and the most difficult. Besides the appendices, you'll find brief "About the play" and "About the scene" descriptions for every single monologue in this book to help you with the context of the piece. However, you shouldn't rely solely on these simple synopses.

To fully understand your character, it's imperative that you read the full play from which the monologue was taken. Many casting directors, adjudicators, and acting coaches absolutely insist upon only working with monologues extracted from a complete play for good reason... character. Reading the larger work helps you more deeply understand the character delivering the monologue. Knowing their arc, understanding their motivations, and having a thorough picture of their relationship to other characters all contribute significantly to help you give the best monologue performance possible.

Each and every one of these monologues is taken from a larger, published work, carefully selected from the broad collection of plays from Pioneer Drama Service. Unlike other monologue books, where it is often challenging to track down a copy of the original source of a monologue, we promise you that every one of these complete plays will always be easily attainable from Pioneer Drama Service, www.PioneerDrama.com.

Yes, ultimately this is just another monologue book. You are not going to read this book end to end and no one will, because monologue books are not really meant for that. So no... it's nothing new or fancy in that regard. But did you notice how many times we referred to this as "unlike other monologue books"? Here you'll find a wide variety of ages, of time periods, of tones, of running times... all taken from published plays that you can find easily on a single website.

Really, what sets this book apart from all those other monologue books is that it keeps you, the actor, in mind so you can find performance material here whenever you need it. We wish you all the best in your continuing journey as an actor. May the monologues in this book bring you great success, whatever your purpose may be.

An Act of Piracy

By Patrick Derksen

About the play: Set in an era when women were not allowed to act and men had to play female roles, Lord Cranbury's traveling company of scallywag actors just can't seem to get their big break! If only he knew that five members of his troupe are actually women… playing men who play female roles. Realizing the troupe's in need of radical revitalizing, Cranbury decides to buy a ship and set sail with his thespian crew. After all, if they are going to do a play about pirates, they should experience the real thing! It's method acting, after all!

Time period: 17th century.

Vivian
30s - 40s

About the scene: The play's opening scene finds the traveling company about to perform locally for the owner of a much more successful troupe. Diva actress Vivian, who everyone thinks is star actor Victor Thatcher, assumes she will be invited to join the more prestigious group. Modest stagehand Jan—the only known woman who travels with the troupe—is saddened to think they might be losing their best actor. Vivian, as Victor, tries to cheer her up by offering her a big opportunity.

Vivian:

You know, don't let them convince you that you've nothing to look forward to besides raising a brood of children. I think you've got a bright future. […]

I've noticed all that you do around here. Oh, you're modest, and that's not a bad quality, but the way you run everything around here, from the advertising to the divvying of the shares—you're the cornerstone of this enterprise. […]

And when Frederica chooses me to be the lead actor of the renowned Gallant Players, I want you to come along with me. My personal assistant! You didn't know I thought so highly of you, did you? Look at you. You're speechless. Yes, personal assistant to the top actor in the country. I tell you this so that you don't get any funny ideas and settle down with some stable boy. You, my dear Jan, are destined for greatness. So let's make this the best show of our lives!

Admissions

By Colleen Neuman

About the play: Evelyn is confused when she wakes up in a strange office. The last thing she remembers is washing the dining room windows. Then Mary, a patient and efficient lady from behind a desk, informs Evelyn that she is dead. She first refuses to believe it. Then, after realizing the truth, she falls apart. After pulling herself back together, she gives an accounting of her life. Within this verbal diary, a few "admissions" are told, parts of her past for which she still feels guilty. The chance to relive one moment allows Evelyn to close the door on her own life, and face, with a sense of serenity, admission to whatever comes next.

Time period: The present.

Evelyn
50s

About the scene: Mary, a business-like representative in the afterlife, is questioning Evelyn and asks Evelyn to recount her sins, starting at the very beginning. In this monologue, Evelyn is on a roll when Mary abruptly cuts her short. This was not to be a laundry list of sins, but rather a test to see if she had a conscience about her wrongdoings.

Evelyn:

My sins? (*A little confidentially.*) All of them? Okay. I'll try… oh.

Wait a minute. I get it. I get what you're doing. You know all about me. All about my family, where I went to school, my babies, this cup, Aunt Syl… (*Smiles a knowing smile.*) You already know all about my sins, don't you? You probably have every single one of them listed in one of those folders. You just want to see if I'll admit to it. That's it, isn't it? […]

(Realizes she's really in the hot seat now.) Okay. Okay. I can do this. *(Up and pacing.)* Let me think back. It was so long ago. *(Thinking hard.)* I was a pretty good kid when I was little. I think. *(Stops. Remembers something.)* Oh! I used to wet the bed. Does that count? […]

(Pacing again.) Let's see, let's see—grade school, grade school. There must be something in grade school. *(Stops. Remembers.)* Oh. Rita Sue. Rita Sue Feiner. *(This is a painful memory for EVELYN, and it shows.)* Second grade. The Feiners moved to town at the beginning of second grade. They were poor. Not that any of us were rich, but we always had clean clothes to wear to school. Not the Feiners. Rita Sue and her brothers always came to school in dirty old clothes—always too big or too small. Nothing ever fit any of them. And Rita Sue was real shy. Never said a word. Never said boo. *(Takes a second, struggles on.)* Nobody wanted to be her friend. Including me. But for some reason Rita Sue took a shine to me. She'd always be looking over at me during class, smiling at me a little. At recess she'd hang around where I was playing. Every time I turned around, there she was, just standing there.

One day I got mad. *(We can hear a little anger in her voice here.)* I didn't like how she was always there, acting like I was supposed to do something about her. So… I did something about her. I said something mean. I don't remember what, but I said it real loud so everybody would hear it. And everybody heard it. And everybody laughed. *(Takes a second.)* Rita Sue looked like she'd been slapped. She didn't say anything, didn't move. She just stood there. She never came around me again. *(This is very real to her.)* I was ashamed the minute those words came out of my mouth. She was so little and so dirty and so poor, and I had to be mean to her. […]

Being a child is no excuse. I knew better. *(Takes a breath. Presses on.)* Let's see… fourth grade. I cheated on a spelling test in the fourth grade. Oh, I could have passed the test without cheating, but I wanted to show off—get a 100. […]

Wait a minute—I'm not done. I'm still in grade school. I didn't even get out of the fourth grade. Wait till I get to high school.

Alive

By Jenny Stafford

About the play: Ashley has given up her career in L.A. to move with her husband for his career. Getting to know their new city, husband Jacob can't resist a good antique store and wondering about the previous owners. But when he arrives home with his latest treasure, Ashley is horrified. He intends for the pretty—but definitely used—urn to hold the ashes of whichever of them goes first. This opens a Pandora's Box, both hilarious and heartbreaking, about their relationship, their dreams, and what makes us truly alive.

Time period: The present.

Ashley
20s - 30s

About the scene: Ashley hints that she's unhappy after moving from L.A. When Jacob pushes the issue, asking if she'd like to move back or even leave him, Ashley finally tells him the truth.

Ashley:

(Finally explodes.) Yes! Yes, okay? I hate it here! I hate everything about this place. I used to have friends and a life and a career. I was doing something I wanted! And now I'm stuck here in this... where even are we?! I'm watching everyone in People magazine live the life I almost had.

I love you—I do, I love you so much, but I just feel trapped here. And when I'm dead, I would like to not feel trapped again. When I'm dead, I would like to feel... alive.

You know you don't even burn to a fine powder when you're cremated? *(Takes the urn from the mantel, slowly lifts the lid, and looks into it gloomily as she talks.)* Some stuff, like your bones and your teeth, don't burn down. So you're just, like, a fine powder full of chunks of who you used to be.

(Beat.) I'm not in the urn yet. I could leave. But... Okay, you know what? I haven't really tried very hard since we moved here. I've just been existing, reading People magazine and eating candy bars and feeling sad. That's on me. Maybe I'm not exactly where I want to be, but... I'm still alive. *(Looks at Jacob mischievously.)* So let's be alive. Let's be alive right now!

◆◆◆

Always Bella

By Kendra Thomas

About the play: The students at Lakeside High don't quite know what to make of Bella, the offbeat and somewhat annoying new girl on campus who tries so hard to fit in when she's so clearly... well, different. But Bella decides that Lakeside's star forward, Katie, is her new best friend, so some classmates cruelly set out to teach Bella a lesson in humility and show her that she doesn't belong in the popular group. Once Bella's brother, Bart, helps everyone understand Bella better by sharing some sobering information about his sister's past, the students realize the dangers of judging a book by its cover and never knowing what's inside.

Time period: The present.

Bella
Teens

About the scene: New girl Bella attempts to make friends during lunch break at her new school.

Bella:

Oh! Nice to meet you, Mia. "Meet you, Mia." I like that. The "m" sound. That's alliteration. I've always liked alliteration. It's such a funny word, too. But not as funny as onomatopoeia. *(Sits at the table next to Katie and opens her lunchbox. Others move away from her, but she doesn't seem to notice or care.)* "Onomatopoeia." Words like "moo" or "crack" or "plop"... or *(Loud.)* ..."bam"!

"Onomatopoeia." *(Chuckles.)* Such a fun word to say. *(To Katie.)* You want one of my apple slices? *(Katie shakes her head and starts to say something, but Bella interrupts.)* I like it when my Mimi packs apple slices. Sometimes she packs celery sticks.

Those are gross. I don't see how anyone could like celery sticks. Even with peanut butter. Who thought that should be a thing, anyway? Who had it in their mind that celery sticks and peanut butter should go with each other? That's just weird. But Mimi packed my apple slices with caramel sauce, so that's good. I like caramel sauce. My brother doesn't. He likes carrots, though. Just raw carrots. I don't guess you put stuff on carrots except for maybe ranch dressing or something, but he likes them plain. Do you like carrots? […]

I don't either. See, I knew we'd be great friends.

The Amazing Majesto

By Brian D. Taylor

About the play: The magician Majesto seems to have stumbled upon some real magic. Through his acutely authentic disappearing acts, he has sent his assistant, as well as a young boy, a prisoner, a socialite, a rodeo clown, and most recently, newlywed Sarah, to a strange void from which they cannot return. As those who've been there longer explain to Sarah of their years in this limbo, the hopeful bride becomes crushed by the realization she may never see her groom again. Yet those who knew Majesto best continue to believe in his magic and hold onto the hope that the conjurer will find the magic to save them all.

Time period: The present.

Blaire
40s - 50s

About the scene: Seeing Sarah's fine wedding gown and realizing she'll never wear fine things or go to parties again, Blaire, a wealthy, entitled socialite, gives the others a dose of the hard truth.

Blaire:

Look at this girl! She's young, beautiful, gorgeous, and all of it is lost! Look at this gown! It's incredible! Perfect lines, exquisite design. Oh, what I wouldn't give to try on a new gown and jewels! And it's not the gown I'm talking about. I mean, sure, I miss the gowns, the jewels, the finer things. But that's not important. Just think of all the simple pleasures you'll be missing now that you're stuck here. Parties, lavish dinners with friends, nights of gossip over cards, the people you love.

That's right, dearies, I do have a heart. I'm not as shallow as you think. And I stepped into that box because no one else would.

Everyone thought it was as stupid as I did, and I should've listened to them! *(Sighs. To Sarah.)* But you see, right?

Sure, I miss all my material things, of course, but I would trade it all to see my friends and family again. Why, even my worst enemy! I'm not angry with them. *(Catches herself.)* Well, perhaps a bit, if I'm being honest—but it isn't their fault. Perhaps the fault is mine. They annoy me because I'm not anything like them. I'm a realist, darling, and it seems certain that our fate has been handed to us and the key has been thrown away. It's no crime of our own, except perhaps for that one. *(Gestures toward Greg, the convict. To Sarah.)* But facts are facts. That door isn't opening again until the next one arrives, until another poor sap is sent here. And I won't mince any words—it's utter hell being forever separated from your life, from the life you once knew, whether that life was one of glorious bliss and riches or one of bitter hardship. That part of it is neither here nor there. It's true I may have been wealthier and better off once, but I can recognize that I'm in the same boat as everyone else here. It's better you face those facts sooner than later. I hope you'll forgive my bitterness about it.

Amelia, Once More

By David Muschell

About the play: This gripping play examines the tension between an actress and the character she portrays. Night after night, sweet Shelly Preston performs the part of wicked Amelia in an off-Broadway hit. The play's success depends on her ability to step completely and realistically into her role. Now Shelly worries that the character is taking over her mind. She wants a night off to regain control over Amelia. However, her unsympathetic director, Alphonse Crevansky, and the ambitious supporting actress, Laura Tontelli, unite to try to convince Shelly to perform. Tom, the leading man in the play, loves Shelly and admonishes her to quit the play altogether, creating yet another force pulling on her.

Time period: The present.

Shelly [1]
20s - 30s

About the scene: In her dressing room, Shelly explains to Laura why she so desperately wants the night off from performing her role of Amelia, before she goes crazy or has a nervous breakdown.

Shelly:

Lately, I've begun to wonder. Generally, when I begin dressing and making up, I have to concentrate so hard to become Amelia… to lay aside Shelly Preston for a while. It's like she's some observer, outside, watching Amelia using my voice, my body. The way Amelia moves, her attitudes, her needs… all not mine!

At first… but not now. In the beginning I was able to slip in and out of Amelia. I could come offstage at the end of the first act and be "Shelly," dressed and made up like Amelia. But night after night... I found I could do that less and less. I had to be Amelia totally or the play wouldn't work. But being Amelia for that length of time... such a horrible woman... she repulses me! If I break character, I find I don't want to return to such cruelty. I have to bury me, the real me, for the entire show every night... every night. [...]

It's like Amelia's taking over, becoming me. I just feel that if I don't stop tonight... it takes me a long time now after the show just to get out of her. You have to have noticed. How I've been acting offstage... [...]

This past week I found myself being "Amelia." At the grocery store, the clerk put something on top of the eggs and I lashed out... or Amelia lashed out. You should have seen his eyes. Walking down the street, at a restaurant... is this what a nervous breakdown is like? Am I going crazy?

◆◆◆

Laura
Late 20s - early 30s

About the scene: Laura, a supporting actress in the play, gives Shelly a pep talk as she struggles with her role playing the ruthless Amelia.

Laura:

Shelly, relax. Loosen up. It's normal for a lot of stress to develop during a long-running show. But, hon, it's what we all want. When you've worked as long as I have... taking this little part here, that role there... just trying to get noticed, get that lead. We've gotten the reviews, the word of mouth. They raved about you, but did you read what they said about me? "Laura Tontelli simpers and cowers perfectly under the brow-beating and whiplike tongue of Amelia." "Perfectly." I went to an audition the other day... for a commercial... and the director said, "You're the one starring with Amelia, aren't you?" Not "Next." I'm getting noticed, Shelly... an overnight success after ten years. [...]

Yes, hon, this life has pressure. You've got to find ways to relax, take it easy—in between the pressures. I can tell you that when a show starts having substitutes for the leads... well, that same word of mouth can hurt you. *(Shelly slumps in defeat.)* Okay, I'm not helping. Did you expect me to say, "Quit. Let this hit go"? You've got talent, girl. Use it. Look, Shelly, can't you just come out tonight with a little less energy? You know, Shelly with just a coating of Amelia? No, really, I know, I know. You'll say you can't play it that way... but it might be a way to get through a bad night. I mean, you can work on this. Find your space in between Amelia. Sooner or later the show will be over, and you can ditch the witch and never see her again.

Shelly [2]
20s - 30s

About the scene: Tom is with Shelly in her dressing room, supporting her desire to take a night off and leave the show to her understudy. Shelly expresses her concerns, relating a childhood memory.

Shelly:

What scares me, Tom, is that if I take one day off, I may never come back. I think Laura and Alphonse believe that. I may run from Amelia and never return. *(Pause.)*

When I was a child, I lived in the country. My father would take us to school in his truck in the early morning mist. And always, dancing in front of the headlights were small rabbits, darting here and there as we drove down the dirt road. Every so often... we'd hit one of those rabbits as it moved too early or too late. I would hear the thump as the tires crushed it. You could feel a small bump. It hurt. A little pain would go through me, and I would shut my eyes. I didn't want to look back and see the small body. I asked my father, "Please don't hit them." I wanted him to swerve or slam on the brakes, but he said that he might go into a ditch or slam us into the dashboard, and that it was better for the rabbit to lose its life than one of us. I didn't argue, but I didn't agree. At those moments, I would have rather lost my life than to have heard that thump again.

Tom, when I begin to "become" Amelia each night, I feel like that rabbit and "she" is barreling down the road straight for me. I wake up the next morning wondering why I'm still me... why Amelia isn't the one opening her eyes... but maybe that'll be tomorrow.

Anne of Green Gables

Adapted by Jody Johnston Davidson

About the play: This heartwarming adaptation beautifully captures the highlights of the classic novel. Siblings Marilla and Matthew are looking to foster a boy to help with work around the house, but quite unexpectedly, Anne is sent to help them. Boisterously loud and bursting with energy, Anne charms the pair into keeping her around. Though she gets into quite some mischief and has many adventures, she touches the lives of all who come to know her and changes their lives for the better.

Time period: 1870s.

Marilla
50s

About the scene: Marilla speaks with her friend Rachel, explaining the task of finding a young boy to help with the chores. Little does she know that the boy she has sent for will soon turn out to be Anne.

Marilla:

Oh, no. I'm quite well, although I had a bad headache yesterday. Matthew went to Bright River. We're getting a little boy from the orphan asylum in Nova Scotia, and he's coming in on the train this afternoon. […]

Well, we've been thinking about it for some time—all winter, in fact. Mrs. Alexander Spencer was here one day before Christmas, and she said she was going to get a little girl from the asylum over in Hopetown in the spring. Her cousin lives there, and Mrs. Spencer has visited her and knows all about it. So, Matthew and I talked it over off and on ever since. We thought we'd get a boy. Matthew is getting on in years, you know, and he isn't as spry as he once was. His heart troubles him a good deal, and you know how desperate hard it is to find hired help. So in the end, we decided to ask Mrs. Spencer to pick us out a likely lad when she went to get her little girl. We heard last week that she was going, so we sent word by Richard Spencer's folks in Carmody to bring us a smart, sensible boy of about 10 or 11 years of age. We decided that would be best—old enough to help with the chores but young enough to be trained up proper. [...]

Today we got a telegram from Mrs. Spencer saying they were coming on the 5:30 train tonight. So, Matthew went to Bright River to meet him.

◆◆◆

Anne [1]
11 years old

About the scene: Curious about her new arrival's background, Marilla has just asked Anne what her story is. Anne declares that the stories she makes up and the novels through which she lives vicariously are much more exciting than her own story. However, she obliges and explains how she found herself in the asylum and ended up at Green Gables.

Anne:

(Sighs heavily.) Well, that is another hope gone. My life is a perfect graveyard of buried hopes. I read that sentence in a book once, and I say it to comfort myself whenever I'm disappointed in anything.

Because it sounds so nice and romantic, just as if I were a heroine in a book. I find my life much easier to tolerate if I can imagine I'm a heroine in a novel. [...]

Oh, what I know about myself isn't really worth telling. If you'll only let me tell you what I imagine about myself, you'll think it ever so much more interesting. [...]

My father and mother were teachers, poor as church mice but ever so in love. I was born to these lovely people. Mrs. Thomas, a neighbor, said I was the scrawniest, homeliest baby she'd ever seen, but my mother said I would grow up to be a great beauty.

Mother died when I was only three months old, and Father passed on four days later. I'm sure it was because he could not bear to be parted from his one true love and not because he meant to leave me alone in the world. Anyway, no one wanted me until finally Mrs. Thomas said she'd take me. I lived with her until I was eight and helped take care of her children. She had four of them younger than me. Then Mr. Thomas was killed, and Mrs. Thomas went to live with her sister, but she couldn't take me. Finally, Mrs. Hammond from upriver came down and said she could use a girl who was handy with babies. You see, Mrs. Hammond had eight children! Twins three times! Now, I like babies in moderation, but three sets of twins…

They meant to be nice people, the Hammonds, but Mr. Hammond drank a great deal, and Mrs. Hammond's temper was short, with that many babies and all. I'm sure that they would have liked to have been… […]

When Mr. Hammond was killed in the mill accident, Mrs. Hammond gave the children up to relatives—they wouldn't take me—and she set off for the States. They almost wouldn't take me at the asylum, but they had to as there was nowhere else for me. Finally, Mrs. Spencer came to bring me to you and Green Gables. You must love it so…

◆◆◆

Anne [2]
Early teens

About the scene: Anne has been with Marilla and Matthew for some time now and has invited her friend, Diana, for tea. During this monologue, Anne repeatedly pours Diana wine instead of cordial, and Diana gets increasingly more intoxicated. Completely unaware of what is happening to Diana, Anne tells this story. (NOTE: […] indicates where Diana interrupts to request more to drink. Each time, Anne pours her more while hardly losing a beat in her storytelling.)

Anne:

Did I tell you what happened last Sunday when the minister was invited for dinner? Marilla thought it would be a nice gesture if we had the minister over for lunch after the Sunday service. She asked me to put the pudding sauce outside on the porch to keep it cool and to be sure and cover the top. Now, I meant to cover it as much as could be, but I had just finished reading "The Crimson Blade"— […]

Anyway, I was very busy imagining the suffering of poor lady Margaret, locked in the tower until her rescue by the dashing Lorenzo. Covering pudding sauce pales in comparison. The next day, Marilla asked me to fetch in the pudding sauce. I discovered, to my extreme horror, that a mouse had drowned in it. I lifted his body out with a spoon—imagine how pleasant it might be to drown in pudding sauce—and threw it out. I washed the spoon, thoroughly, five times. Marilla was out milking, and I meant to tell her, but then I got involved pretending to be a frost fairy, turning the trees red and yellow. […]

Then we were off to church and back again, and the minister was here and we were all enjoying lunch, and then the next thing

I know, Marilla is walking out with the plum pudding in one hand and the pitcher of warmed up plum pudding sauce in the other. Diana, that was a terrible moment.

So, Marilla cut a large slice for the minister and covered it with the tainted sauce. I wrestled with my conscience. He raised the fork to his mouth and... and... I leapt up in my place and shrieked, "Aaaaah! You mustn't eat that. A mouse drowned in the pudding sauce!"

Bad Dates

By Jon Jory and Michael Bauer

About the play: Jill and Greg grew up together and have been happily together since Greg awkwardly tried to kiss Jill in the fifth grade. But a dozen years later, the sparkle in their relationship has dulled for the two young 20-somethings. They reluctantly agree it would be good to see other people. When their dates turn out to be narcissists, manipulators, obsessives, and imposters, the couple realizes you sometimes don't appreciate what you've got until it's gone.

Time period: The present.

Katy
20s

About the scene: Greg is on a first date with Katy, who is clearly a basketball player because she's wearing her basketball uniform and high-top sneakers. So far in their conversation, Katy has shared that her nickname is Ka-ching, but she was unimpressed when Greg shared that he likes to play badminton.

Katy:

Say, badminton-guy, do I smell?

I get the impression you are smelling me in a negative way, which is quite hurtful and demeaning.

So, Greg, let's be frank and honest with each other as the basis for any relationship we might establish between you, teeny-tiny racquet guy, and myself, mainstream sport athlete of the female gender. I mean, what you do is fine, but you probably don't work up a sweat, whereas I play an actual sport and sweat like a pig, and I need to know if a little honest sweat would, like, prevent you from showing up on our wedding day because my smell offends your badminton nostrils, thus embarrassing me in front of my family and coaches? [...]

What do you think we are doing here? Laying out your itsy-bitsy badminton court? You didn't ask if I wanted to "hang out," you asked if I would be interested in a "date," which is one step from "I do," and I said, "Yes, I would," and high-tailed it over here, skipping my twenty-minute cold shower, which is crucial to my post-game cool-down, allowing you to see me in my game uniform, which I never usually do until the third date. So, Greg, we are either on the road to a lifetime of wedded bliss or we are over—done, defunct, extinct—or to put it another way, toast? [...]

You are breaking up with me?! I can't believe you! *(Stands up and claps her hands for attention.)* Excuse me, foodies. This guy, Greg Whosis, lured me out here to Pork Chop Heaven under false pretenses, has intimated that I smell, and after all my sacrifices to try and make this relationship work, is dumping me in this incredibly public way and preventing me from having the two perfect children and late-model Subaru I deserve! Thank you and eat up. *(To Greg.)* Well, Greg, I spit near you. *(She does.)* I don't spit on you because you don't deserve my spit, Greg, you are a selfish, disloyal earthworm of a man who leads a girl on until you finagle her into Pork Chop Heaven where she is thoroughly disrespected and... *(Speaks to the whole restaurant.)* ...it is my hope that some real man in Pork Chop Heaven who is not a badminton player stands up for me, Ka-ching, and mashes this guy's nose like an Idaho potato rolled over by a sixteen-wheeler! *(Storms off.)*

◆◆◆

Beautiful

By Shawn Deal

About the play: Gabrielle is blind, but has tremendous insight. Troy can physically see, but doesn't notice much. When Troy first approaches Gabriella at the park and tells her she's beautiful, he's taken aback that she rebuffs his compliment. He's even more surprised when he realizes that the young woman is blind, yet still appreciates beauty all around her.

Time period: The present.

Gabrielle
Late teens - 20s

About the scene: Gabrielle explains to Troy how she experiences beauty.

Gabrielle:

Yes. You're like most people, viewing beauty as something you see with your eyes. But when you can't see, it doesn't mean you don't understand it. You have to feel beauty instead. My life is made of feelings more than anything else. I enjoy a beautiful moment every time I wake up. It's the feeling of being alive! Beauty, to me, for me, is much more an experience... like being here in the park. Before you came, I was sitting on the bench listening to the birds sing. If I listen close enough and long enough, I feel like I can almost understand what they are saying. I imagine the conversation the birds are having. If it's just one bird, I can hear the song it is singing and, sometimes, I can even mimic it—the whirring sound of the hummingbird, the noisy chirp of the blue jay, or even the buzzing of a bee.

Baking cookies is another beautiful experience. Mixing the ingredients together, listening to the eggs crack and the milk pour, feeling the dough stick all over your fingers, rolling it into little balls, licking your fingers when you are done... *(Imagines it.)* There's nothing like raw cookie dough! And then waiting the minutes as the cookie dough bakes, and the cookies form their round circles. But it's the growing smell that gets me the most. At first there's nothing, except maybe some excess flour floating in the air—enough to make you sneeze! But when it comes to baking, the smell of warm cookies just grows and grows, starting with a very faint aroma and growing until it fills the entire kitchen, and then the whole house.

There are so many simple things I find beautiful— the sound and smell of sizzling bacon, a child's laugh, music— Oh, how I love music! A warm breeze on my cheek, walking barefoot in the grass, listening to crickets and frogs at night... sitting on the porch and feeling the air change temperature from day into dusk into night.

It's exhilarating! Sitting by the ocean, listening to wave after wave come in. Burying my feet into the warm sand...

And I believe that the world, as I perceive it through my senses, is much more beautiful than the world you see with your eyes.

Bedlam and Breakfast

By William Prenetta

About the play: Alan Barton has one successful Broadway play to his name. Now, if he can write a hit movie script in just one week, he just might reignite the flames of his fame—and of his failed marriage to Hollywood starlet Sylvia Belmont. His chances look good when he books a secluded beach cottage where he can focus on his writing. But eccentric landlady Mrs. Lombardo seems to suffer from memory loss and has triple-booked the bungalow! The stonewalled scripter finds himself sharing the small space with a doddering auntie with her teenage chatty niece Susan and her friend Millie, as well as a secretive Russian woman "from Detroit" and her even more cryptic comrade, who dresses like a Cold War spy! While the Russians lurk suspiciously, Susan proves to be most troublesome, introducing to the crowded house a biker gang and her boyfriend's band! Poor Alan is up to the gills in chaos… and then his ex-wife Sylvia shows up!

Time period: 1959.

Millie
Teens

About the scene: Susan has been sneaking out of the cottage and asks her friend Millie to cover for her. Millie's attempt to do so is quite poor when Alan asks her why Susan is gone.

Millie:

Oh, please. Oh, please, don't make me tell you, Mr. Barton. I promised I wouldn't tell a soul, cross my heart and hope to die. You're not going to make me tell you, are you? […]

She's out with a boy. Oh, my goodness. I just told you. And she met him the day we got here. His name is Johnny. I think it's true love. At least that's what Susan thinks. Oh, no. I just told you. She's going to murder me! And if her aunt finds out, she's going to ring-a-ding my ring-a-ding. What is wrong with me? Maybe it was the Russians. Or the whiskey. I accidentally took one sip. I found it here in the kitchen. [...]

It may have given me a hangover. But I'm not sure because I've never had a hangover before. And then, Susan and I buried the bottle under the lifeguard tower. Are you going to rat me out, too?

Big Boys Don't Cry

By Vern Harden

About the play: This powerful, haunting drama portrays the devastation of child abuse and the often complex story behind it. Fifteen-year-old Lenny Barnes has been hospitalized and his mother, Ethel, and her husband, Guy, are on trial for child abuse. Simple flashbacks show the events leading up to the fateful night as Lenny struggles to be accepted at school, at home... in life. His parents flounder, caught in the web of poverty and frustration in their marriage that is filled with both love and hate. The play balances well the drama of the courtroom scenes with the action and violence of the flashbacks.

Time period: The present.

Ms. Roberts
30s - 40s

About the scene: The prosecuting attorney gives her opening remarks to the jury in regards to the child abuse case against Ethel and Guy.

Ms. Roberts:

(Addresses the judge.) Thank you, Your Honor. *(Turns to face the jury [audience] and addresses it directly.)* Ladies and gentlemen of the jury, the case you are about to hear deals with one of the most vicious crimes which exists in our society today—that of child abuse. It is vicious for several reasons. First, it involves the violation of every human's right to freedom from fear, to the right of protection from pain and suffering, both physical and mental.

Next, it is doubly vicious because it involves the inflicting of pain and injury on one who is helpless in every way—a child. It is vicious because it damages not only the mind and body, but because it damages the spirit, the soul, the very essence of what makes that individual. And for this injury, there is no repair. How does one go about restoring the shattered faith of a child? How do you undo the fear and mistrust of not only the offending parent, but of every adult, everyone in whom trust should be placed, every authority figure encountered for the rest of that child's life? Ladies and gentlemen, how do you undo... hate?

The defense attorney in this case is my distinguished colleague, Mr. Wayne Lee. He is an experienced lawyer, a brilliant debater, and in this instance, completely wrong. No matter what he says, no matter what he makes you feel, remember that violence has been done. And if our children are to be free to live, this violence must be stopped. The prosecution will prove, beyond doubt, that such abuse has taken place, not once, but repeatedly. Ladies and gentlemen, there is no way to repair damage already done. But what we can do is see to it that those who abuse children never have a chance to repeat those acts. And that is what the State is asking you to do. Find the defendants guilty. Give them the punishment they deserve. Help us protect our children from abuse. You must find these defendants guilty. Thank you. *(Returns to her chair.)*

◆◆◆

Ethel
32 years old

About the scene: On the witness stand, Ethel tells her story in what becomes a heart-wrenching monologue in response to questions from both the prosecution and the defense. It begins when her husband jumps up from the defense table at the prosecution's insinuation that Ethel was a prostitute when Lenny was an infant.

Ethel:

I couldn't find a job at first. My baby was hungry! *(Screams.)* What did you want me to do? *(Breaks down crying.)* I didn't have any place to go. I couldn't find work. So, when this man offered me money, I said, go ahead. *(She pauses to regain her composure.)*

There's a lot of things a person can stand in this life, if she has to. But one thing no mother can stand is seein' her baby go hungry. When you look at it that way, doin' what I did wasn't so bad. You think about that before you go passin' judgment.

I finally got me a job where I could earn regular money. Times wasn't easy, but we made do. Later on, I married Ronnie. I worked at the plant with him. He was killed in a car wreck when Verlene was just a baby.

Two years ago, I met Guy. I was lonesome. He was lonesome. Lonesome people are good for each other, Ms. Roberts. You know what I mean? I didn't even know how lonesome I was until Guy started comin' home with me.

After we got married, I quit work because that was what he wanted. But money don't last long when you've got kids to feed. Guy'd get upset. Lenny was growin' up, gettin' harder to handle. That's when I started drinkin' again. It wasn't a problem at that time. It was when I was workin' the streets. Some of the men I took home weren't very nice. Drinkin' was the only way I could stand them, or me. It helped me get through the nights.

I went to A.A. for a while. They were good people. Only then I'd have to leave the meetings and go home. Nothing changed there. I'm not a very good person, I guess. I'm not strong. I'm not much of anything.

Guy was a good, loving man. He liked the children. And they liked him. It was nice to have a man around again. He was strict, even with me. But that's all right. It lets a person know they're loved. If a man didn't love his wife, he wouldn't care what she did.

But, you see, Lenny was growing up. Fast. Faster'n we wanted him to, I guess. Guy was a proud man. And Lenny was growing up just like him. Mr. Lee, two proud men in the same house don't always get along. Can you understand what I'm saying? I've got two men in my life now—a husband I love and a son I love. But they see things differently.

Can't they see that we all want the same thing? All I've ever wanted was a safe, quiet place to be with the people I love!

I'm sorry. I did everything I could to make a home for both of them. But nothing I did was ever enough. Mr. Lee, when all a person's got to give ain't enough, what is there left to do?

A Bowl of Soup

By Kendra Thomas

About the play: Certain foods connect us to our past, to our family, to meaningful life moments. The smell of something cooking—even something as basic as a bowl of soup—triggers memories and speaks to us in a way that nothing else can. In this soul-warming drama, five teens share what their unique bowls of soup mean to them.

Time period: The present.

Milly
16 - 18

About the scene: Milly explains how chicken soup became so important to her.

Milly:

My mom always had to get creative with food. She had two jobs—one during the day and one at night just to make ends meet for five kids—which doesn't exactly lend itself to the grandest of dinners. But somehow, she always managed to make it fun. We ate breakfast for dinner for a whole week once. Pancakes, eggs, cereal. She made it sound exciting, and we didn't know it was to save money. We were being adventurous, eating Beanee Weenees or hot dogs with mustard for a meal—hot dogs without buns, of course, because that would cost more. I was a lot older before I realized we were—as my school put it— economically disadvantaged.

When I got older, Mom put me in charge of dinner so that she could work more and go to school at night. You know those big cans of soup? Not the little single servings but the big family size cans? Well, I'd get three of those big chicken noodle soups and heat them in a pot on the stove to feed us all. It became my favorite go-to dinner. So when my mom asked me what I wanted for my birthday and told me I could I spend $10 on whatever I wanted... I looked up a chicken noodle soup recipe online. I planned my budget down to the penny!

Somehow, we made it work. I made a whole pot of chicken soup, more than ever came from all those cans, and for my birthday, we stuffed ourselves with homemade chicken noodle soup.

Over the years, I've made that soup a bunch for my family. I can actually make it for cheaper than the cans you buy at the store if I plan it just right. Mom asked me once why I like making it so much, why it means so much to me. For me, it just goes to show that you can get by on something simple... like canned soup. But you can also make it better yourself and in the process, make yourself better.

My mom graduated with her bachelor's degree last year. She's got a great job now, and she's home with us every night. We've learned to make a lot of homemade meals... but I still make chicken soup every single Friday.

The Boy with No Name

By Ev Miller

About the play: Eddy is a very special young man. Blessed with a healthy eighteen-year-old body and a winning disposition, he is also developmentally disabled, having the intellectual capacity of an eight-year-old. Kathy, his mother who wrestles with guilt over Eddy's condition, retreats into the anguished world of abusive behavior and tranquilizers. A visit by Eddy's Aunt Paula almost ignites this volatile situation into a family tragedy. There are no easy answers, but Eddy himself suggests a way to help overcome their problems and rebuild the family.

Time period: 1980s.

Kathy [1]
Mid - late 30s

About the scene: Eddy's mom, Kathy, speaks candidly with her sister Paula. She confides that she suspects her husband, Allen, is seeing another woman. She knows he doesn't love her anymore and only stays at the house because of Eddy. Kathy thinks about institutionalizing Eddy to ease her burden and try to save her marriage.

Kathy:

Paula, Allen is in love with another woman. […]

(Nearly out of control.) How do I know? Oh, a woman can tell. More trips than usual, hanging up the phone just as I enter the room, little looks that are there or not there the way they used to be. Phone calls here that never hang up when he answers but always do when I get to the telephone first. […]

(Screams.) No! I am not imagining things! I'm losing the only purpose in my life... the only thing I care about... he doesn't love me anymore. The only reason he stays here is because of

him. *(Laughter, shrill and irrational.)* Isn't that a scream, Paula? The reason my life has gone to hell is because of... him... and yet it's the only reason my husband stays with me. But, don't you see, Paula, that if it weren't for him the way he is, our marriage would be the way it used to be? Just the two of us... Allen and I.

(Pacing again.) Paula... I've been thinking. I've been doing some checking. There's a school upstate... at Grafton, that takes people like him. They can teach him to do some jobs to support himself. I... I just can't face the thought that he will be here... my responsibility until the day I die. I just can't face that.

(Calmer.) I mentioned it to Allen just once, a few weeks ago. He was furious. He said he wouldn't hear of it. He said he couldn't send his own son away to an institution. *(Looks at Paula.)* Why, even Dr. Karstan says it wouldn't be a bad idea. He says the reason I'm so nervous all the time is because of... the situation.

(Angry, turns away.) You think I'm crazy.

Kathy [2]
Mid - late 30s

About the scene: Eddy's mother, Kathy, speaks candidly with her sister Paula. Paula insists she should see a psychiatrist to help her cope with having a mentally disabled son, but Kathy does not think anything will help at this point. She is plagued with guilt that Eddy's condition is all her fault because he was born out of wedlock.

Kathy:

What good would that do? Would a psychiatrist be able to make my son normal? Would he be able to make my husband love me again?

(Almost pleading.) Because it's not my fault! Don't you understand that? Why doesn't anyone understand that? *(Again, she slips back into an irrational voice.)* I tried to be a good mother. I tried to make up for what I did. When he was just a baby I cared for him... I sat up with him when he was sick. I dressed him nicely. It's just that as he got older he started to destroy everything. When he plays with other children, I'm worried sick that he's going to be too rough. When we have company, I'm afraid he's going to do or say something to humiliate me. Paula, you're the first company I've had in this house for three years. Everyone is embarrassed by him. They feel sorry for me. They pity Allen. I can hear what they're saying to themselves. "Why did this happen to such a nice couple?" "They seem to be so decent." *(Laughs.)* They don't know, do they, Paula? They don't know that the nice couple conceived him in the back seat of a car!

(Hysterical now.) Paula, you remember what Mama used to tell us, don't you? That girls who do that before they're married end up paying the price? I didn't believe her. I didn't even believe her when I had to get married. I didn't believe her for a lot of years... but, by God, I believe her now! I believe her now!

But I'm Only Seventeen

By J. Don Luna

About the play: This award-winning socio-drama has a number of scenes dealing with current problems facing today's young people, such as sexually transmitted diseases, date rape, suicide, and distracted driving. Because of the broad number of topics it covers, the play is ideal as a discussion starter. The scenes don't offer or force solutions and are not at all preachy. Instead, this moving drama provides an avenue for groups to discuss critical issues which affect teens' lives.

Time period: The present.

◆◆◆

Mary
17 years old

About the scene: Mary and Doris are spending time with their friend Susan, who hasn't been herself since she was raped recently. Doris has just encouraged Susan to tell people what happened, but Mary vehemently disagrees. Mary, too, has been raped, and since no one ever believed her, she is sure no one will believe Susan either. Still, Mary understands Susan's pain and comforts her, offering to help her tell her mother or someone—anyone—who can listen and understand.

Mary:

(To Susan.) She can't! No one would believe her! I know! Of course I care, but I also know that no one will believe her!

Doris, listen to me, it happens a lot... and it happened to me, too! No one cared about me! No one believed me! They said that I must have been drunk, and I must have asked for it. My older sister said to keep my mouth shut and just learn to forget about it. That it happens all the time. And just forget about it! Susan, what do you want to do? I believe you. I just... You didn't do anything wrong! It wasn't your fault. I know how you feel. So ugly and hurt inside. So betrayed. Would your mother listen? I'll help you. I'll go with you. This has got to stop. No one should have to go through all this shame and guilt. We have got to stop hiding this. If you can't tell your mom, then we'll tell the nurse or the school counselor or your minister until someone listens who understands...

She
17 years old

About the scene: He and She have been dating for a while, and He is ready to take "the next step" and finally have sex. She responds to him by stopping his advances short, wanting to know that it is right, safe, and worry-free. She wants to talk things through before they make love, knowing they will respect each other the next morning.

She:

There are a lot of things I need to think about before I make a decision to make love with you. There's more to love than just telling someone that you love them. I need to feel comfortable here. I need to feel comfortable making a decision like this. I need to know that it's something that I want in my life... not something I feel pressured into. I'm just saying that we need to think about this. There are many things to consider. You know what happened to Bill and Bridget. They felt that they had to get married. Getting pregnant is not the reason I might want to get married. And then there's the problem of sexual diseases... With AIDS and some of the other diseases that are out there today, all it can take is one time. *(He starts to say something.)* I know that you respect yourself, but can you say that about everyone you have ever been with? And everyone that they have ever been with? Even nice people can make mistakes. I just don't want to do something that I might regret later. I don't mean to accuse you of anything. I just need to make sure that I do what I feel is right at a time when I feel comfortable. I need to know that it is right for me. I don't know if I'm ready for this yet.

I don't know... I just know that I want to be able to look myself in the mirror tomorrow and say that I love and respect myself and I need to love and respect YOU, too. I need to know that I can depend on you to allow me the right to make my own decisions in my own time, and that you will respect my choices. Isn't this something worth waiting for? Isn't this important enough to feel good about? This is an important decision, and I want to know that we're both mature enough to feel right about this and to be reasonable about the choices that we're making.

(After a moment of silence between them.) I want you to know that I do care for you, and I want us to make good choices about important decisions that could affect us for the rest of our lives. I think that sex should be something special, and that it's worth waiting until both of us are ready for it. Aren't I worth waiting for? I think you are.

Camp Stowaways

By Tracy Poverstein

About the play: This delightful coming-of-age fantasy has fun exploring the "right" age to give up sleeping with stuffed animals and blankies. It's summer break and a group of tween girls are about to face their fears and insecurities as they learn to cope at Camp Libertas, where they'll find only tough love, not loveys. Major Marjorie and Miss Angie aim to lay down the law and turn another group of girls into young women.

Time period: The present.

Major Marjorie
30s - 50s

About the scene: Major Marjorie was once a camper at Camp Libertas. Now, she is the unforgiving camp director who has no problem enforcing the strict rules of the camp in an unyielding manner. As the campers sit around the campfire one night, she tries to toughen up the girls—by telling them a ghost story!

Major Marjorie:

That's right, campers, I know the joys of Camp Libertas firsthand. When I was a young cadet, the camp included boys, and there was a boy here named Eric Mueller. I'll never forget that name. He had the bluest, kindest eyes I had ever seen.

One night our camp director sat with us around a campfire, much like this one, and warned us not to leave our cabins in the middle of the night. For safety, he said. Then, we all retired to our cabins for the evening.

The next morning, no one could find Eric. The boys said he had left the cabin to look for his flashlight back at the campfire. All morning, we searched for Eric—behind every bush and rock. It wasn't until we looked up into the trees that we saw poor Eric Mueller draped over a tree limb... dead! We never discovered who—or what—had gotten to him.

(Beat.) Okay, sleep well, campers! Tomorrow is the scavenger hunt, and the camper who finds the most things gets her Darwin badge. Remember, the nearest hospital is 200 miles away, and I sleep with ear plugs, so... nighty-night. Caw, caw!

The Canterbury Tales

By Burton Bumgarner

About the play: Chaucer's literary masterpiece revolutionized English literature. Tossing in a good helping of Monty Python-styled humor creates this incredibly silly yet educational comedy. You'll meet many of the pilgrims whose tales are most likely to be studied in high school... along with a few Thanksgiving pilgrims that ended up in the wrong play!

Time period: 1300s.

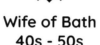

Wife of Bath
40s - 50s

About the scene: One of Chaucer's pilgrims, The Wife of Bath is a headstrong, pushy woman who now sells DVDs on "successful husband training." She considers herself an expert on the subject, having had five marriages.

Wife of Bath:

(Enters carrying a DVD case, a stack of paper, and an instruction manual.) Before I begin my tale, I shall speak at length on the subject of marriage. *(Holds up the stack of paper.)* This should only take about 45 minutes.

I am an expert on the subject of marriage. I have gone through five husbands—three of my husbands were good, and two were not so good. I learned the best thing to do with a husband is to rein him in and get him under control. You must do this early in the marriage, or else the window of opportunity will be past and you will be stuck with an unruly brute who burps out loud and leaves his dirty socks on the sofa.

I have developed a 12-step program to help women to take control of their husbands and their lives. It's called "The Wife of Bath's

Guide to Successful Husband Training." Each step is presented in an easy to understand and entertaining 120-minute DVD.

Now, I will send you the first DVD absolutely free. If you are not at least 50% satisfied, then you may return the DVD at no obligation. If you are at least halfway satisfied, then you will receive a new DVD every week for the next 12 weeks for the low price of $19.95 per disk. In my first lesson, you'll learn all about whining and nagging and making his food so spicy he can't eat it. And if you order today, you'll receive... *(Holds up manual.)* ...my "Wife of Bath Teach Yourself Karate in Three Weeks" manual absolutely free. Not only will you be able to nag your husband into a quivering mound of Jell-o, you'll make him afraid to leave the basement. So, take out those cell phones, turn 'em on and call this number. *(Gestures to indicate a phone number.)* Have your Visa or MasterCard ready. And now, I'd like to spend some time telling you about each of my marriages.

Cirrius, Nebraska

By Nick Vigorito, Jr.

About the play: The town of Cirrius is so small that the mayor is also the judge and the postmaster. But the secret the townspeople hold is no small one, as a New York businessman discovers on a trip to the Brigadoon-like town. After a few meals with the locals at the bed and breakfast, the Stranger soon finds that while warm and kind, nobody can take a joke. Through a string of comically awkward interactions with the tight-lipped townsfolk, the secret behind the serious mood comes out… it is against the law to laugh. When Rose, the local school teacher, tells the Stranger about the fateful day the bizarre law went into effect, a glimmer of hope for change creeps through the gray clouds that have been hanging over Cirrius for years.

Time period: The present.

Rose
20s

About the scene: The Stranger is on his way to Omaha to meet up with his business partner. Making a stop along the way, he finds himself in Cirrius, Nebraska. The Stranger is both confused and unnerved that all the people are so nice, and yet they are not allowed to laugh. Here, Rose explains the reason for the law against laughing.

Rose:

The legend is that when the Native Americans lived here years ago, they used to look out on the horizon and they would see these beautiful cloud formations—these soft, white, billowy pillows of heaven. They believed that these breathtaking works of art were created every day just for them… a different masterpiece every day. They used to draw the cloud formations on rocks. To this day, photographers and artists still come out here to look at them. Photograph them, paint them. They say that they are unlike any other cloud formations in the world. So beautiful. So unique. And that's why early settlers gave the town its name... cirrius, like the cloud. [...]

I wrote a poem once... *(Emotional.)* ...called "Cloud Heaven." [...]

There's a lot you don't know. [...]

I mean about us... the town.

My dad wasn't always the mayor. It just seems as if he was. He used to drive the school bus that picked up all the kids. He loved it. And the kids loved him. He would tell jokes and stories. All the kids couldn't wait to go to school, just to get on his bus. Well, one day about 20 years ago, my dad drove all the kids in the grammar school to a class trip—an old gold mine just outside of town. My mom volunteered to chaperone it. It's about a half hour ride, and the whole way there my dad was telling stories, jokes. The kids were laughing. My dad dropped my mom, the teacher and all the kids off at the mine, and he went to go park the bus. They had only been inside the mine about a minute or two. My dad heard this awful roar. He ran back to the entrance, but it was too late. There was a cave-in. The entrance was completely blocked with rubble. He heard their screams. He ran back to the bus to call for help, and then he ran back to the entrance. He tried to dig it out with his hands. He still has scars. There was nothing he could do. By the time help arrived, it was too late. My mom, my little brother, the teacher, and the 25 other kids on the bus all died that day... in one fell swoop. Every single child from our grammar school died. All but one... me. I was sick that day. I didn't go on the class trip. I stayed here... *(Gestures inside.)* ...with Maggie. I was supposed to be on that bus. [...]

My dad nearly lost his mind after that. He probably would have given up if it weren't for me. All he kept saying was how he had a busload of wonderful, beautiful, laughing children one minute, and a minute later, they were all gone. All he kept saying was how he couldn't stop hearing their laughter. The whole town died that day. We were never the same after that. A few of the parents took their own lives. There wasn't a reason to laugh anymore. I'm sure that must sound strange to you, but nobody laughed for so long after that. The town was never the same. How could it be? My dad became mayor and revitalized the town, not only financially, but in other ways, too. It was years before anyone smiled, let alone even thought of laughing. And then after a while, it just seemed wrong to even want to laugh. Somebody brought it up at a town meeting, and the next thing we knew, it was a law. I guess out of respect for all the lives that were lost—the lives that were forever changed—nobody really brings it up anymore.

You probably think we're all crazy. Right? [...]

I used to go there, and I would sit for hours and look at that mine and then out on the horizon. I couldn't understand how the same God that could create such beautiful clouds could let that happen to all those innocent children. It was on one of those days that I wrote that poem, "Cloud Heaven."

Diary of Adam and Eve
Adapted from Mark Twain's *Diaries of Adam and Eve*
By Sam Birnkrant

About the play: Adam and Eve discover each other in the Garden of Eden and record their experiences on stone tablets. Eve tries to knock down a few stars to wear in her hair, discovers the beauty of fire, talks to her reflection in the pool thinking it's her sister, and pleads with Adam not to go swimming over Niagara Falls. At last, however, when they leave the Garden, Adam and Eve discover their enduring love and need for each other.

Time period: The beginning of time.

Eve
Young adult

About the scene: On her first night on Earth, Eve takes in the stars and the moon.

Eve:

I am almost a whole day old now. Yes. Now what? *(Scribbles with stone.)* I arrived yesterday. It's best to start right and not let the record get confused. Some instinct tells me these details are going to be important to the historians some day. *(Drops the stone, gazes.)* I feel exactly like an experiment... just an experiment, and nothing more. Everything looks better today than it did yesterday. *(Looks around approvingly, then rises and stares off into the distance.)* Except in the rush of finishing up yesterday, the mountains were left in a ragged condition. And some of the plains were so cluttered with rubbish that well, everything was done too hastily.

For instance, *(Looks up at the stars.)* ...there are too many stars in some places and not enough in others. And the moon got loose last night and slid down and fell out of the scheme. It's a very great loss. Breaks my heart to think of it. It should have been fastened better. If we can only get it back again... But, of course, there's no telling where it went to. And besides, whoever gets it will hide it. I know it, because I would do it myself. *(Returns to rock, sits, resumes carving her diary with stone.)* I do love moons. They are so pretty and romantic. I wish we had five or six; then I would never go to sleep.

(Glances up toward the stars, then scribbles with stone.) Stars are good, too. I wish I could get some to put in my hair. *(Excitedly.)* Maybe I can! *(Jumps up, picks up a pole. Standing tiptoe, she tries to knock down a star.)* Oh, darn it! They're higher than they look! I know what... *(Drops pole, picks up a stone.)* I'll knock one down! *(Throws. Another. A third stone. Then, disgusted.)* It must be because I'm left-handed or can't throw well.

(Frustrated, Eve weeps. Then brightens.) I know what! I'll pick stars closer to the ground. Then I can gather them with my hands and won't have to break any of them. Of course! What an idiot I am! *(Reaches for stars. Can't make it.)* It's no use. They're farther than I thought. I'm pooped. Can't drag my feet another step. How'll I ever get home? *(Shivers.)* And it's turning cold.

(Suddenly.) Oh... there's a tiger! You know, I've never seen a tiger before, but I knew him in a minute by the stripes. Wish I could have that fur... it would make a lovely coat.

Disorder in the Court

By Brianna Dehn

About the play: Casey Licit is on a cross-country road trip when she's apprehended and held for trial in a town appropriately named Berserksville. Charged with an outrageous triple crime, Casey maintains her innocence. But as the trial begins, our level-headed defendant realizes her hapless defense attorney is an ineffective dolt, and the prosecution effectively uses silly, childish distractions to win the case, including bribing Judge Falter and witnesses with candy and leading the courtroom in the Macarena!

Time period: The present.

Glen
20s – 30s

About the scene: Faulty witness and town gossip, Glen Chatter, is on the witness stand, giving the lowdown on what went down… except it's not even remotely about what went down.

Glen:

Glen Chatter, town gossip. I am the ears of the town. Nothing happens without me hearing about it. *(Looks around suspiciously and leans in.)* You want to know the lowdown? The word on the street? Well, I know this guy, who knows this guy, who knows this guy's podiatrist, and this is what I heard.

If you go to the lower eastern west side of town, and turn into the third alley you see, not the one with the dog who knows how to play the harmonica, the next one, and enter in the back of the building with no windows that vaguely reminds you of a low-budget horror movie, at the door will be a one-eyed, three-armed man named Ambiguous Pete, who will give you a very indifferent answer on whether you can enter or not.

Enter anyway, and if old Pete comes after you, ask him about his childhood. That will send him running for the hills, because confrontation is his biggest fear, right after snakes and losing a game of Monopoly.

Once you are in the building, it will give you a weird feeling, like when you see your teacher outside of school, or when you find out one of your friends is distantly related to Henry the VIII. Don't let this stop you, and you will find a woman with her fingers superglued together and bright blue eyebrows, but not above her eyes, sitting in the corner. Tell her "The geese fly south in the winter, it's time for them to come home." She will nod, and that's when you can get your Hannah Montana CDs.

Door to Door

By Flip Kobler and Cindy Marcus

About the play: Two doors onstage represent various types of doors in life: bedroom doors, closet doors, apartment doors, dorm room doors... even the metaphorical doors we face every time we make a decision. Individual scenes take us through these doors, offering a breadth of tones that reflect upon life, choices, moments, and self-discovery. These scenes are punctuated with a series of monologues that collectively tell Trish's story, starting from when she's a young girl to when she becomes a woman, a wife, a mother, a survivor, and a widow.

Time period: The present.

Trish
5 years old, late 40s, and mid 60s

About the scene: Throughout the play, we see Trish at various stages in her life. The monologue below brings together three of Trish's scenes, from when she is a young child to when she's a mother and finally to when she is a widow. The three parts of this monologue can be presented in whole or any part can be presented individually.

Trish:

(Five years old and in the middle of a tantrum. Slams a door.) Jordan! Jordan, Jordan, JORDAN! Eeewwwwww! *(Flings open the door and screams out.)* It wasn't my fault! Jordan did it! He's the one that needs a time out, not me! *(Slams the door.)* Stupid Jordan, always getting me in trouble. I just want to pinch his little head. *(Opens the door and screams out again.)* You can't keep me locked in my bedroom! That's child endangerment, and they'll come and take me and put me in a foster home, and you won't ever find me 'cause lots of people are called Foster so you'll never see me again! *(Slams the door, really loudly this*

time. *Opens the door and yells.*) I didn't mean to slam the door. (*Slams it again, even harder.*) I wish Jordan was a Foster so I'd never have to see him again. (*Drops to her knees.*) I hate you, Jordan! And I will for as long as I live. Cross my heart and hope to die, you are my enemy forever! (*Flings the door open and yells.*) It's been five minutes! (*Marches out through the door, closing it behind her.*)

(*In her late 40s, talking on the phone.*) Jordan, please... Yes. I'll hold. (*Paces.*) ...Jordan? Hey... Yeah. I heard from the doctor... I'm gonna need the surgery... Hysterectomy... No, no, she thinks the tumors are benign, but she's not sure... Yeah, everything has to come out. (*Fighting back tears now, trying to be brave.*) Sooner rather than later. So I guess this means no trip to Nepal?... Yeah... Right, who wants to go to Nepal when they can go to the hospital? (*Cries.*)... It's just this was supposed to be JoJo's graduation gift... and now I've ruined everything! (*Gets it under control.*) ...What? No. I know he'll understand... Yeah. You're right. We can always go after we get him through college... Huh? You're coming home? But... no... Yeah. I love being home with you, too, except your camping trip... What?... Well, yeah. I just wouldn't ask you to give that up, too... You'd rather?... Really? (*Starts to cry again, but this time for different reasons.*) ...I love you, too... Okay, I'll wait here for you. (*Gets her tears under control.*)

(*In her mid 60s, holding an urn that contains Jordan's ashes.*) Oh, Jordan. I miss you, babe. JoJo says I should spread your ashes over the Himalayas. He says he'll take me, but I don't want to go without you. It was gonna be our thing. Stupid cancer. (*Starts to cry.*) God, I hate this. I don't want to spend the rest of my life without you. Who's gonna make me fruit salad? And tell me it's gonna be okay and make me laugh? I can't do this, J. I can't. I'm not the strong one. And now I have to be. *(Gets a hold of herself.)* So, ah, I guess, I should go back in there. JoJo says it's cool. Being a widow gives you certain perks. *(Starts to cry again.)* I don't want perks! I hate perks! I want you here. With me. Growing old together. Holding my hand. But, once again, you're exploring exotic places ahead of me. *(Smiles. Looks at the urn as she realizes what she's just said.)* Oh, my love. You are, aren't you? Oh, babe. I hope it's amazing for you. Hey, Jordan? See ya. *(Leaves the urn and slowly closes the door behind her as she exits.)*

Dracula

Adapted by Stephen Hotchner

About the play: Jonathan Harker has been warned by Dr. Van Helsing, his close friend and world-famous scientist, to be wary of his trip to Transylvania to close a real estate transaction with Count Dracula. But Harker is young and ambitious. He stumbles into a web of terror that nearly sends him to his death. When Harker escapes Dracula's clutches, Dracula follows him to England, knowing who his next victim will be: Lucy Wenstrom, best friend to Harker's wife, Mina. Harker and Van Helsing are unable to save Lucy from Dracula, who then turns on Mina. To break the spell, Van Helsing and Harker return to Transylvania, trying desperately to discover Dracula's whereabouts. The coach breaks down. The wolves are baying. A night of terror begins and all nearly lose lives and souls.

Time period: 1890s.

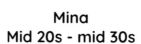

Mina
Mid 20s - mid 30s

About the scene: Mina tells Dr. Van Helsing that she is concerned about Lucy's change in behavior.

Mina:

You will not believe what I am about to tell you. But I beg you to listen, all the same. Have you noticed something peculiar about the way Lucy is acting? […]

It began three days ago. There had been a great storm. A storm greater than any the local fishermen could ever recall. Boats were smashed against the large rocks that ring the harbor. Waves climbed to record heights. There was panic among the tourists on the beaches. Then, out of nowhere, a ship appeared on the horizon. And at that very moment the tempest broke. Then there came a fog, a mass of dark mist which seemed to close on all things like a grey pall. We were on the East Cliff, right at this very place, watching it all. Something... not human... came with that ship. I'll never forget Lucy's face as she watched that ship race toward the harbor, as though, at that moment, some spirit was communicating across the sea to her. And then that corpse, which swung horribly to and fro at each motion of the ship. Even the panicked tourists were entranced at the sight of that dead man, lashed to the helm. We saw that poor dead Captain lashed to the helm of his ship, and I heard Lucy whisper, "thrilling, absolutely thrilling." It was like listening to a stranger. She even seemed upset by this cross I wear.

Lucy talked about that ship for hours. Then it began. The sleepwalking. My room is next to Lucy's. I remember hearing her toss about that first night, moaning so despairingly that I went into her bedroom to see what was wrong. I couldn't wake her. Her eyes were open and she cried out, "Yes, master, I am here." Then she went back to sleep. I never did wake her. […]

It grows stranger. I heard her get up the next night. I followed her. She walked by the curved path to the stone bench where we now sit. The moon was full. She stood at this place, her eyes fixed upon the sea. She stood so still... Then she raised her arms to the moon as though she were embracing something or someone... invisible. I raised my eyes to the moon to see what she was looking at. I saw a bat hovering over Lucy, not more than twenty or thirty feet in the air above her. […]

That was yesterday. I took my late afternoon nap and when I woke the sun had gone down and Lucy was gone. I came here. There is an old stone monolith. You see it there? […]

I hid behind it and watched. I saw Lucy on this bench. Then, as though out of nowhere, a tall dark stranger sat down beside her. Lucy had a book of poetry in her hands and the stranger took the book from her. She turned toward him as though hypnotized. I called out, "Lucy, who is that?" Then the stranger whirled and glared at me. I shall never forget those eyes, red and gleaming in the dark. Then the stranger turned and vanished, vanished into the night. I called again, Lucy turned toward me, smiled in a way I will always remember. And she said, "Why, who could you be talking about, darling Mina?" [...]

I tell you, her life is in danger. I can feel it. And I need no science to tell me that Lucy is possessed. By what, I don't know, but I do know she is not the Lucy Wenstrom once called my best friend.

The Empty Chair

By Tim Kelly

About the play: At a group counseling session for teenagers recovering from substance abuse, there's an empty chair. One of their peers, Robert, has just died of an overdose. Accident or suicide? The atmosphere is tense and uneasy. Finally, each young person speaks about their memory of Robert. The dramatic monologues tell us a great deal about each speaker and the terrors of drug abuse. Although Robert remains something of a mystery, his impact on the others is undeniable. This is a hard-hitting work with an emotionally strong anti-drug message.

Time period: The present.

Speaker #5
Teens

About the scene: One of Robert's support group members, a street-wise philosopher, opens up about her complicated friendship with him.

Speaker #5:

Okay, okay, we play by the rules. *(By rote.)* My name is [supply first name]. I'm [supply age]. I'm a recovering substance abuser. I only had one friend. I only wanted one friend. I only needed one friend. Crack. You could keep your liquor and your nutritious food and your nice warm home. If I could smoke crack I had it all. I mean—ALL.

Or thought I did. I wasn't afraid of anything. Until—until—

—until Robert told me I was afraid. Boy, did I laugh at him. Then, he spelled it out for me. Like a teacher writing something on a blackboard. Said I was afraid of coming down. Said I had to keep my head twisted 'cause I couldn't stand myself when I was clean. That shook me up. Honest. Sounds simple but I never looked at it like that before. When I was smoking, everything looked different. No problems. When I wasn't smoking, I was always scared. The days when I couldn't scratch up some money were—well—I felt like I was living in hell. I felt like my skin was on fire.

Know how I got to this place? Robert brought me. He didn't stay. I turned around and he was gone. And I thought to myself, "Boy, Robert knows what it's all about. One very self-contained dude. Nothing will get him down. He'll beat the odds."

Last time I saw him he said he was joining the Marines. Didn't matter that he was underage. He had "ways."

He always talked about his folks. He made them sound like they were rich and famous and beautiful. Funny thing, though. He never seemed to go home. He was always—"around." Someplace, somewhere. I think Robert understood a lot about other people. But I'm not sure he understood himself. Maybe he didn't see enough of the world. Or—maybe, he saw too much.

Or, something like that.

Fighting for My Self

By Renee J. Clark

About the play: Pressure to be thin. Pressure to be popular. Pressure to have sex. Pressure to do drugs. All of these are very real stresses on teenage girls, many of whom lose their way just trying to survive. This full-length drama is an intense portrayal of these situations as the characters struggle to win back their self-reliance and hold on to their identities in the face of peer pressure. Though focusing on women's issues, this poignant play is vital for all, offering a message of hope.

Time period: 1990s.

Juanita
Teens

About the scene: Juanita delivers this eulogy at the funeral of her best friend, Tanya. Tanya was killed by a gang member in a random shooting.

Juanita:

This is really hard for me to do. *(Clears her throat, holding back tears.)* Tanya was my best friend since we were four. When I think of her, I think back on the many years of friendship and love she has given me. I guess I can't believe she is really gone. That she won't be here to pick me up when I get down. I can't believe she won't be here when I want her to be the first to hear a new joke. *(Laughs bitterly.)* She always laughed at all my jokes, even when they weren't funny. But that was Tanya. She liked to make you feel good. And how she loved to laugh. She always saw something funny in everything, no matter how negative a situation might be. I can't believe I won't hear her laugh again.

Tanya was a gentle person. Did she ever say an unkind word about anyone? Never. She never judged people by their looks, and she tried to be friendly to everyone, even the kids no one liked. She was always there to help you, if you needed it. Tanya was the only one I know who used to hang out at the homeless shelter. She'd volunteer once a month to serve soup. Some of you thought she was crazy going down there. But she once said to me that being with the homeless reminded her of how lucky she was to have a home, food, and a family that loved her. She said that everyone needed to be reminded of that now and then. She felt we needed to give a little of ourselves to those less fortunate in order to find out who we really are. At the time, I didn't understand what she meant. But now that she's gone, I think I do.

Tanya loved all things and believed everything in nature connected. I remember once when we were in third grade and walking home from school, we came upon a big spider dragging itself around the gutter. Two of its legs were missing. Tanya scooped it up with a paper and carried it home in her lunch box. She was going to feed it and nourish it back to health, then let it go. A spider of all things! By the time we got it home, it was already dead. I remember how sad and disappointed she was. She insisted we give it a little funeral in her backyard.

The last few days have been a nightmare for all of us. Nothing makes any sense to me anymore. I only know we are hurting. I only know her death is wrong. It's not fair that someone like her should die so young... and so violently! I wish I could bring her back, for all of us. *(Stops, unable to go on.)* Thank you.

◆◆◆

Kim
18 years old

About the scene: Kim has read the diary of her younger sister, Allie, and discovered that she is addicted to hard drugs. Kim is only 18, and having been through treatment and detox herself, she is afraid for her little sister. Allie is showing all the signs of hard drug use—loss of appetite, doing poorly in school, and spending loads of time with Brad, a dealer whom Allie is dating. Kim tries to intervene by talking to Allie.

Kim:

(Impatient.) Will you listen to me? They've discovered that addiction might be hereditary. It runs in families. I've apparently inherited the tendency to become addicted to things, especially chemicals. Remember, Grampa was an alcoholic... and so was Uncle Jim. In treatment, I learned the younger you are, the greater the chance for addiction. *(Earnestly.)* Allie, you may have inherited this tendency, too. Maybe you haven't.

But can you afford to take the risk? *(Silence. Continues quietly, gradually building in emotion.)* I read your diary not because I wanted to pry or be nosy, but because I don't want to see you destroy yourself like I almost did. I want to spare you the agony of withdrawal, the paranoia that everyone is against you. I don't want you to lose all your real friends, the ones that really care about you. I don't want you to cause Mom and Dad more pain like I did. I don't want you to lose yourself and maybe never find it again. I don't want you to hit rock bottom and then cry for help when it might be too late!

And I don't want to lose my little sister and never get her back.

I tried to die, Allie. There was nothing to live for. If it wasn't for my best friend, Jenny, ratting on me to Mom and Dad, telling them how bad I really was, they might never had gotten me the help I needed before it was too late.

Liz
Teens

About the scene: Liz has not been happy since her parents' divorce. Her mom has tried to cheer her up by reminiscing about good times in the past, like jumping in the leaves and sharing about the day over milk and cookies. In this monologue, Liz responds to her mom, angrily describing what her depression feels like and how difficult it is to get through a typical day.

Liz:

I don't know what's wrong! *(Stares at her mom for a moment.)*

All right. You win! Then will you leave me alone? *(Mom nods yes. Liz begins a huge tirade that reaches its peak as she finally attempts to make her mom, as well as herself, understand her depression. Throughout, her tone is bitter, sarcastic, and angry. She paces as she tries to vent her frustration.)* Okay. You want to know what's wrong? You want to share my day? Get out the milk and cookies, Mom, 'cause you asked for it. A typical day in the life of Elizabeth Carrington. Let's see... what should I start with first?

I know. *(Pointedly.)* Since you're never here when I get up, how about I start with the morning, Mom? *(Mom reacts with a guilty nod.)* Okay. Every morning I dread the start of a new day. I am so exhausted, I don't have the energy to move. You see, I don't sleep much at night, Mom. I spend the night either crying or gazing into darkness, wishing I could become a part of it. In the morning, when the alarm goes off, I just stare at the clock, listening to its awful hum that has robbed me of my solitude. I watch the seconds flash by, wishing I could go back to sleep... forever. But somehow I force my body to move. I'm on automatic as I go through the motions of getting ready for school. Sometimes I don't even know what clothes I put on... not that it matters... not that I care. I usually skip breakfast since I don't have the energy to make it. The school day is a blur in slow motion. I float from class to class, avoiding eye contact with everyone. If I just sort of look at the floor, nobody can see me. In class, I'm usually in a kind of daze... or else I sleep. Most of the time the teachers don't even know I'm there. They seem to look right through me. I ask myself, why am I here? What is the point? Why bother? I am alone... but I don't mind 'cause it's safer that way. Sometimes I'll meet some of my friends behind the school during lunch. I don't really like them much, but they usually have something to drink.

Don't look so surprised, Mom. Drinking and drugging go on all the time at school. The teachers are just too stupid to see it. And, yes, I drink. I drink 'cause it dulls the pain that comes from trying so hard not to cry. It's actually a physical pain, Mom. When I hold back my tears, my face feels like it's stretching tighter and tighter until the skin is going to pop loose. And my throat slowly twists into a knot and tries to choke me. But the booze helps to numb the pain, and it fills me with... something... and just for a moment, I am not an empty shell anymore. *(Sits, pauses, and attempts to go on.)* After school I come home to this empty house... and the pain returns.

Then when you finally get home, all you do is bitch at me. So I turn on MTV, nice and loud. It helps to drown you out... and... *(Sarcastic.)* it helps me to forget my wonderful day. *(Laughs bitterly, then turns to Mom.)* There. Are you satisfied now?

Sometimes I feel like I'm going crazy, like I'm going out of my mind! I want to crawl into a hole somewhere and curl up into a tiny speck in the dark and disappear. *(Starts to weep softly.)* And you know what, Mom? I hate it all. I hate the way I act at school. I hate the way the guys are. I hate the way my friends are.

And I hate the way I treat you.

And I hate the way I can't jump in the leaves anymore.

Marcy
Teens

About the scene: Marcy is in the hospital after she has been brutally beaten and raped by her boyfriend Mike. She is talking with her friend Sylvia and divulges the story of what she remembers from the vicious attack.

Marcy:

You were right. I should have broken up with Mike months ago. Then maybe this wouldn't have happened. Things haven't been good between us for about four months. Mike would go into rages of jealousy over nothing. He'd accuse me of cheating on him if I even looked at another guy. It was like I was being suffocated by him. He resented any time I gave to anyone else... my family, school, even you. *(Wincing from pain.)* But you don't know how hard it was trying to break up with him. Every time I'd bring up the subject, he'd whine and say how much he needed me, that I belonged to him, and he wouldn't be able to go on without me.

Yesterday we finally had it out. We were walking through the park on our way home from a party. Mike had had a drink or two, so I figured he was mellow enough to try again. I told him

I couldn't stand the pressure anymore, that I didn't want to see him for a while. He... he went crazy. He went out of control. I know he's got a bad temper, but I've never seen him lose it like this. He scared me. So I tried to walk away... but he grabbed me and started shaking me. *(Begins to weep.)* When I tried to run, he... he... tackled me and punched me, first in the face. I tried to scream, but he hit me again, and again... and again. I started to black out just as he... *(Sobs.)* he... oh, God...

He raped me! I thought I was going to die. He was like a monster.

I don't remember anything else. I woke up here. How could he do this to me? I thought he loved me. *(Pauses, catches her breath.)* The police were here. I told them everything. What do you think they'll do to him?

Fosters

By Kendra Thomas

About the play: This sweet, touching play explores the special connection between abandoned animals in need of homes and foster children who often feel alone in this world. Playwright Kendra Thomas beautifully gives everyone—human and animal—a voice to tell their story.

Time period: The present.

Anna
Teens

About the scene: Anna is meeting Isabelle, the house parent at the children's home, for the first time. The clothes Anna wears are too big, her shoes are scuffed and dirty, and her hair looks unkempt. With Isabelle frozen, Anna steps forward and addresses the audience, sharing how she was abandoned by her mother and is now in foster care following the death of her only other caretaker, her grandmother.

Anna:

I always thought you had to be an orphan to end up in foster care. Like not have a family at all. But I still have a family. I've never known my dad, but my mom... well, I don't remember too much about living with her. I was really little. She had a hard time taking care of me because "she has problems"—that's what my grandma used to say. I used to live with my grandma. It was because my mom was struggling with her problems. So, one day the police came where I was living with my mom, and then my grandma picked me up and took me home. I was five then, and I'd been with her ever since. It wasn't perfect, because she was old. She couldn't run around and play with me like a lot of my friends' parents played with them. And when I got older... well, let's just say she was old-fashioned. She didn't really understand kids. But it was okay. We had each other, and it was home.

But when Grandma got sick, they started looking for relatives who could take care of me. They brought in a social worker, and I told her that they just needed to find my mom, that she'd come get me. I knew she had problems, but we could make it work. Right? The social worker just smiled and said they'd do their best. Grandma kept getting sicker, and I had to stay some nights with a few of her friends until...

(Can't bear to say it.) After the funeral, the social worker came and got me. She explained that my mom... my mom didn't want me. Or maybe she couldn't take me. But she never came to tell me herself, so I really don't know. And now? Now I'm here with Ms. Isabelle. *(Looks off at Isabelle and smiles, then turns back.)* This has been home for three months now. There's a family that visits me. They went to church with me and my grandma, but I didn't know them that well. Now, they say they want to adopt me. They want to give me a new home just when I'm getting used to this one. My grandma left me. My mom left me. My dad left me before I was born... How am I supposed to trust a new family? I think I'd rather just stay here, where I don't have to get close to anyone and I feel safe.

The Gift

By Virginia de Wyze

About the play: Five women, in turn, come into possession of an ornately carved wooden box: a naïve young housewife, a charming grandmother, a misguided social climber, and a singularly untalented singer named Ivy looking for her first big break.

Time period: The present.

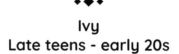

Ivy
Late teens - early 20s

About the scene: Ivy, seeking a big break and a few dollars, visits her friend Chester, who owns a pawn shop in New York City.

Ivy:

Hi, Chester. How ya doin'? Say, I like your new sign. It's all lit up. I could see the words, "Chester's Pawn Shop" blazin' three blocks away. Real fancy. Business must be good. […]

Ha! What new job? Let's just say I'm between jobs, again. Yeah, I got fired from that one, too. I haven't worked in two weeks. I'm really tired of them crummy jobs that won't do nothin' for my career, anyway. I come all the way to New York City to be a singer, and all I've done is go from one lousy job to another just tryin' to stay alive. Can I help it if I have to leave work for auditions? I tell each new boss that the job is only temp-a-rary... *(She has trouble pronouncing all big words.)* ...on account of my singin' career, and all they say is, "Yeah, sure, kid," and then I get fired for takin' time off.

Looks like ya got a lotta new stuff. Boy, when I make it big, I'll come in here as a payin' customer and buy ya out. […]

Ha! Yeah, I know I always say that. But it won't be long now. Hey, would ya look at that bracelet!

Sna-z-zy! That's too lux-ur-ious to be sittin' in a pawn shop. Pretty soon I'll have all kinds of bracelets like that, and I'll never have to come into a pawn shop again. Oh! Nothin' personal. [...]

What have I been doin' with my time? Thought ya'd never ask. One of my gentlemen was talking over my singin' career with me the other night and gave me this tip that the singer at The Top Hat Club quit, and he says if I get down there maybe I could have the job. Then he told me this guy to see there and, Chester, this'll kill ya, the guy that owns the place, see, is also one of my gentlemen friends. Ain't that somethin'? There were three other singers at the auditions, yesterday, so he says he'd let us know, but I know I got the job. [...]

How? It's simple. First, I'm a good singer. Second, he likes me. And, third, now that I know his real last name, there's just a simple matter of a phone call to his wife. [...]

What do ya mean? It's not either a dirty deal. It's business. You see, Chester, this is my first chance at the big time. I've never been this close before. The pay ain't that great, but I'll get what they call ex-po-sure. The Top Hat Club is a class place. They got them neat red and white tablecloths, and I hear that some of the beer is even imported. Ya can get a clean glass with each round if ya ask for one. They even got this big guy hired that does nothin' but stand in the door and sees no un-de-sir-ables get in. By workin' there, I'll probably meet some classy people like maybe a talent scout, and then I'm on my way. So, now I gotta get all dolled up with a new dress for my de-but, but I'm kinda short on cash. So, I says to myself, it's time to visit

Chester's Pawn Shop. What do ya mean, don't my gentlemen pay me enough? Just what kind of a girl do ya think I am? I only take the money when I'm des-per-ate. [...]

Say, quit askin' all them questions. I'm here on business. Look what I got. *(Takes a box out of a tote bag.)* How much you gimme for this box? No, it ain't hot. It's an heir-loom from my dear departed mother. It's been in my family for years. I hate to give it up, but I do need the cash, and this is the last valuable thing I own. Look, hand carved. It's in great shape. Probably one of them collec-tor's items. Sixty bucks? Is that all? Chester, I thought we was friends. [...]

Oh, yeah, I did say this was business. Okay, okay, I'll take it. Thanks, Chester, you're a doll. Where did I really get the box? Hey, honest, it ain't hot. I found it about a year ago in an alley behind one of them fancy hotels uptown. Someone musta threw it out. It was just layin' in the alley so I took it. Honest, it's the truth. Anyways, it was someone's jewelry box, and I used it to keep my tips in from them crummy waitress jobs. Well, I gotta be home to answer the phone when The Top Hat Club calls. By the way, I'll save ya a table up front any night ya want. Hey, Chester, I forgot to tell ya. I have another new show biz name. Because The Top Hat Club is so nice, I thought I'd need a so-phis-to-cated name. How about ... now get ready for this... Ivy! Kinda neat, huh? Just like all them big stars who only use one name. Wow, I can see it in lights now! Ladies and gentlemen... The Top Hat Club proudly presents... Ivy!

◆◆◆

Grover

By Joel Fishbane

About the play: At its core, this layered one-act is about learning what you truly want. Wife separates from Husband while she decides if she wants to leave him or not. Knowing how much he hates dogs, she decides to get one to make sure he stays away. The problem is that Wife hates dogs, too. After all, their mutual hatred of dogs is what brought the two of them together in the first place. Wife finds herself in a deal with Gibb, an employee at a unique pet shop, who arranges for her to become the owner of a fictional dog named Grover. Considering the dog doesn't really exist, it begins to cause Wife a lot of serious problems which escalate quickly.

Time period: The present.

Wife
20s - early 30s

About the scene: Wife sits on her favorite park bench as she shares her surprise with the audience at how many people believe that her fictional dog, Grover, is real. The lie is so well-anchored that no one in her life doubts it. She is extremely proud of herself.

Wife:

People are amazingly gullible. Everyone knows about the Spanish Prisoner. Someone comes to you and says he needs help paying the ransom of a wealthy man in Spain. You give him money in exchange for the hope of being rewarded once the prisoner is freed. In modern times, the prisoner comes from Nigeria. And it's not always a prisoner. Sometimes it's an expensive artifact or a lost suitcase of gold. You pay to secure its release. And of course you never hear from the con artist again. This is a very old scam. Most people know it for what it is. Yet the scam continues, which has to mean that it works, that there are enough fools in the world to make it worth the time.

People ask me about my dog all the time. Not a single person is in doubt. This makes me more successful than all the con artists in Nigeria. I guess it's because nobody thinks you would ever lie about owning a dog. Those are the best lies. Don't tell people fantastic stories about Spanish prisoners. You have to give them something they can believe. My parents sent me money for dog food. Five hundred dollars so I could buy Grover something nice. They're very excited. They never liked my husband, so they endorse anything that keeps him away. My mother even bought me a subscription to Dog Fancy. I feel bad, but I really like the articles. This month's issue has the history of the dachshund. It's pretty informative.

High-Rise High Jinks

By Kenneth R. Preuss

About the play: This one-act consists of five short, comedy duet plays, each taking place in a different apartment in a high-rise complex.

Time period: The present.

Dawn
Early 20s

About the scene: College student Emma's plan for a quiet night reading *Great Expectations* is interrupted by her new roommate, Dawn. Seeing Emma's book stirs all kinds of stories from Dawn.

Dawn:

What's the book? Great Expectations? My English teacher assigned that in high school. Twelfth grade. Spring break. It was awesome! Killer condo, all-night parties, third runner-up in a blindfolded shuffleboard tourna— […]

Planned to read while I tanned, but used it as a coaster for my Sunrise Surprise instead. We should drink one together sometime. It's orange juice and tequila, but I got a special recipe from this one-eyed Hawaiian woman I met in an aban-doned mall.

I hate writing. Actually, had a Great Expectations essay due after spring break. Met a cute guy dressed as a leprechaun at a St. Patrick's Day party who wrote it for me. Scored pretty well. To be honest, the end of senior year was kind of a blur. Finding a leprechaun isn't always lucky. That's a story for another time, though.

(Sighs.) I need to read more books. Or a book. This is why you're in college and I'm in... *(A realization.)* ...terrupting. I'm sorry. *(Moves back to the chair.)* I'll let you finish. Or get started. Restarted.

◆◆◆

Hush

By Kendra Thomas

About the play: As dusk falls on a secluded pecan grove in the farmlands of the Texas countryside, two best friends meet at their secret childhood hiding place. Haunted by memories that have led them to this moment, the girls hash over old times, seeking to understand their past and the secrets they've held for so long. As Gwen faces the reckoning of her own suffering at the heavy hand of her grandfather, Katie tries to reconcile years of turning a blind eye to her friend's obvious anguish and the entire community's sense of propriety that silenced those who cared.

Time period: The present.

Katie
19 years old

About the scene: Katie returns home from her first year in college, eager to reconnect with her childhood best friend, Gwen, who still lives with her abusive grandfather. As they stand amongst the trees, Katie recollects the time when, as children, they discovered the hidden grove, led by a firefly that Gwen thought was her grandmother.

Katie:

I remember the moonlight the evening we first came here together. We followed a lightning bug, but you told me you thought it was your grandmother that led us here. I always thought that, too. The memory of what she did for you seemed to light the way, as though after she was gone, she wanted to show us a place to hide, a place to disappear into the night. We laughed all the way here—do you remember? And finally, just as we arrived, you caught that firefly in your hands. We looked up and gasped at the sight of the twisted limbs of the pecan grove, curled over us like her arms once curled over you. [...]

I remember you telling me about her. How she sheltered you in the midst of his fury. How she locked you in your room. [...]

And you told me you just knew she lived on here with the angels. [...]

And I thought it was so poetic! I thought it was a flowery artistic comment—beautiful and terrible—but I never did anything to help you. [...]

And now here we are again, surrounded by your angels. Listen to the heavenly chorus echoing through the trees. Does it pierce your soul? Do you know that every piece of me is lying broken on the forest floor right now?

I was just a child! I didn't know how to speak then. But I'll speak now. Tell me what to say.

If These Walls Could Talk

By Robert Swift

About the play: This insightful play confronts the problems of today's youth with honesty and forcefulness. Elaine, now a successful author of a self-help book, returns to high school five years after graduation to receive an award. Through her memories, we meet a fascinating gallery of recognizable young characters. The timeless issues of high school students are addressed head-on while retaining an upbeat and positive outlook.

Time period: The present.

Gloria
Teens

About the scene: Gloria is the most popular girl in school—boys love her, girls want to be her. Speaking at a school assembly, she boasts about how her popularity gives her a sense of self-worth. She shares her secret that no matter what, she smiles. It's clearly part of her charm and popularity and helps her not care about the people who don't like her.

Gloria:

Hello. For those of you who don't know me, I'm Gloria Russell. I'll probably be voted most popular girl at James Madison High School. In the yearbook. I think that's quite nice. I'm not downgrading the others, you understand. "Best Combination of Beauty and Brains"—"Best Looking"—"Most Sociable"— "Sweethearts Forever"—"Class Wits"—"Objecting Always." It's just that being popular is important to a person's sense of worth. I'd be less than honest if I didn't admit some people don't like me. Yes, I know it's hard to believe. But it's true.

It doesn't worry me, though. Not in the least. Early in life I discovered a wonderful secret. I discovered how to sail through the storm of living without being affected by it. The winds and the hurricanes of existence pass me by.

Whenever I don't understand something. Whenever I don't know how to answer a question. Whenever there's something I don't like—I smile. *(Smiles.)* When you smile, people think you're being charming. One of the nicest things about smiling is that you don't have to think about anything much. People will always think you're interested in what they're saying. Whenever I'm at a loss for words, I smile. I think the ability to smile is a gift. I feel true pity for people who can't smile. I believe deeply in the words to that old song—"Let a Smile Be Your Umbrella." There's a lot to think about in those words.

Let a smile be your umbrella. That way no one can rain on your parade. *(Silence. Gloria appears to be lost deep in thought. Then, she smiles.)*

◆◆◆

Rose-Marie
Teens

About the scene: Rose-Marie is not bothered by stereotypes and gender rules. She just asked Stanley to prom—he said "no," but only because he does not wish to wear a tux instead of his varsity jacket. Here, Rose-Marie talks to a friend on the phone, wondering if there's anything wrong with being assertive and aggressive.

Rose-Marie:

Can we talk?

I am seriously worried about my future. I am worried about my personality. Everyone tells me I'm too assertive, too aggressive.

They say people don't like that. They don't mean "people." They mean men. The male animal does not like a female animal who is assertive and aggressive. Tell that to the lioness in the jungle. The male lion doesn't seem to mind. I mean, like, what am I supposed to do? When I see something that needs to be corrected, I correct it. When I know a question has to be asked, I ask it. Why put me down for that? Am I expected to go through life with my mouth shut and my ears open? I might as well wear a veil. I tried it once—being meek and humble. Didn't work. Wasn't me. I've got problems. I don't want humankind to think I'm a geek. You know what really worries me?

Am I going to go through life hoping the Stanley Browns of this world will ask me for a date? I'll have to give this some serious thought.

◆◆◆

Teen Elaine
Teens

About the scene: In this flashback scene to when she was in high school, we see that Elaine is not a popular girl and struggles to be included. She has just run into Gloria, the most popular girl in school. Desperate to fit in, Elaine offers to make decorations for an upcoming party the popular clique is having, hoping to be invited. Rebuked by Gloria, the teenaged Elaine then rants to the audience.

Teen Elaine:

(To Gloria.) I'm good at decorations. I'd love to help. Honest. I can do wonders with crepe paper. *(Disappointed.)* Oh, I'm sorry. I didn't mean to intrude. Sorry, sorry. *(Calls after Gloria.)* If you're planning on cutting any more classes just let me know and I'll take notes… *(Faint.)* I don't mind… honest.

(Rage mounting, she practically screams.) Auuuuugh! *(Slams books on the bench, turns to audience.)* What is the matter with me?! I did everything but crawl. What's so terrible about trying to be friendly? It wouldn't hurt Gloria to invite me to her lousy party. I'm not a leper. I wouldn't steal the frosting off the cake. They think I'm a waste of time because I take school seriously and they don't. They think they're twenty years old, and I'm ten. At least I have enthusiasm, and they don't. All they can do is smirk and make smart remarks. *(Chin up.)* Someday I'll show them. They'll be sorry. *(Calls after them.)* Just you wait and see! *(Picks up books.)* Just wait.

If Gloria Russell came up to me this minute and said, "Elaine, would you like to come to my party?" I'd look her straight in the eye and say—"yes."

In the Hood

By Pat Lydersen

About the play: The corner of 159th Street and 43rd Avenue is a lively neighborhood. Kids play hopscotch while the shop owners take care of their businesses. But kind, old Mr. Fineburg is in money trouble and about to lose all the buildings he owns thanks to Mr. Guy Jantic. The greedy businessman is threatening to purchase the properties and turn the street into a state-of-the-art parking lot. Mr. Fineburg's tenants, who are also his friends, get together with other residents to try to save their "hood." It looks like they're doomed to failure until modern social media saves the day.

Time period: The present.

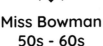

Miss Bowman
50s - 60s

About the scene: Ditzy, eccentric Miss Bowman is a long-time resident of the neighborhood who constantly reminisces about her days on the stage while teaching acting to many of the neighborhood kids and teens. She is currently leading an outdoor acting class in her very unique, extravagant, and dramatic style.

Miss Bowman:

Now, children, as I told you before, we will be filming this class so my unique methods of teaching the grand art of acting will be recorded for posterity. That means that the generations which come after us will be able to look at this film and understand the unique genius I employed in passing on my acting techniques. *(To Jimmy.)* Focus on me during most of the filming, James. I am, after all, what this film is all about.

Now, children, spread out so you'll have plenty of room to work. No more talking! It is time to emote! Everyone imagine that you are an ice cream cone—cold, rich, and creamy with a lovely crisp and sugary cone.

You love being an ice cream cone! Think of what flavor you are. Chocolate? Strawberry? Or perhaps a tasty butter pecan! Become that ice cream cone, children! Glory in your cold creaminess! Glory in it!

But, oh, what is this? It is beginning to get warmer. You are starting to melt! Oh, yes! Melt, children! Melt down the sides of your cone, which is becoming soggy and soft! Sink slowly to the ground, sink, sink! Close your eyes. All is black!

Now, you are trapped in a tight, leathery shell. You are a butterfly in your cocoon ready to emerge! Push against the wall of that cocoon! Push! Push! Finally, you are out. Fly into the sky! You feel free and happy! Flit through the air! Flit, children! Flap those wings! But then… a storm comes up. You are tossed back and forth in the wind. Back and forth! Back and forth! What are you to do? What are you to do? You fall to the ground, your wings twisted and broken!

Then, slowly, something magical happens. You begin to grow! You grow up, up, up, to become a giant oak tree. Be that oak tree, children! Feel your branches and your leaves rippling in the breeze. Feel the sap coursing through your veins! You are strong! You are powerful!

Julian

By James Janda

About the play: This play is a dramatic monologue based on the life of Julian of Norwich. Writer, mystic, and anchoress, Julian is the first known English woman whose written work survives. A contemporary of Chaucer, Julian lived during the Hundred Years War and survived three outbreaks of the Black Death and the division of the Holy Roman Catholic Church.

Time period: Early 1400s.

Julian
60s

About the scene: This monologue begins the play and finds Julian sitting in her anchorhold, attached to Edward Church in Norwich, England, speaking with Margery Kempe, another famous woman from the same time period. Margery is fearful that Julian's insistent reference to the Holy Spirit as "Her" could be considered heresy. In return, Julian fears that Margery's vow to be chaste while married is not what God intends in a marriage. Margery insists her chastity will bring her closer to God.

Julian:

Yes, Margery, I understand.

There are tempests

and storms,

and howling winds,

and hail and ice,

but they too shall pass—

The Holy Church—a what?

A ship of fools?

But Margery,
if you image it
a ship—

I beg your pardon,
I was not listening?

A "leaking" ship
of fools—

Yes, Margery, I have seen
a few fine paintings
depicting it as such—

No—

But—
That is quite true,
none has depicted it
as a "leaking" ship—

You are quite right,
none has done thus—

I?
I see it more
as a nest—

Yes, a nest—

No, not a hornet's nest,
a bird's nest,
a robin's nest—

Yes, it was meant to protect
the fledgling soul
until it is ready to fly—

Now who might the mother bird be?

No, not the pope,
nor bishop,
nor priest—

No, none such as me—

Think, Margery, think.

You have seen her pictured—

Close, not the dove,
but whom the dove symbolizes,
God's Holy Spirit—

Yes, I did call the Holy Spirit
"her."

Yes, I know, everybody
is suspected of heresy
these days—

Yes, I am careful.

I'd never say "her" to confuse
a priest or bishop—
only to women such as we—

Yes. That is our joke.

What, leaving so soon?

To see a White Friar?

Who?

Brother Anthony?

Brother Anselm?

Brother Joseph?

You can't recall his name,
but he abides at—

Brother William,
Brother William Sowfeld.

He confirms you in your
vow of chastity? But
what of your good husband?

He objected at first, but
has since succumbed to
the Holy Spirit?

But Margery, married life
with husband and children
is not lechery.

You say chastity is a more
perfect way. I beg to disagree—

Did not our Maker
wish such? Seeing as he fashioned us
thusly?

Oh, you have a heaven-sent
confirmation of it?

A stone and piece of
wood beam fell
down from the ceiling
of the church and struck
your back while at prayer—

And you are here to tell of it.

Yes, but what has this
to do with denying your
husband by new vows?

Oh, a sign from God.

You ought to
remain chaste?

Now how does that follow?

I am not tired—
I quite follow you.

Yes, I have seen several
people today.

What? Oh, bless you. Bless you
for the wine and bread.

Godspeed, Margery,
Godspeed you, Margery Kempe.

Advice and ghostly counsel!
If I have said fair words,
they come not from me,
but—

From God—
God, our mother.

Yes, Godspeed.

Yes. I shall be careful.

Yes. I know they are burning heretics.

It is still early in the day!

◆◆◆

A Lass Unparalleled

Adapted by Paul T. Nolan

About the play: Adapted from Anton Chekov's Swan Song, Lola, an aged, successful stage actress, finds herself alone in the theatre one night after a performance. While she is feeling sorry for herself, she meets and is comforted by Hedda, the theatre's cleaning woman.

Time period: 1960s.

◆◆◆

Lola [1]
58 years old

About the scene: Lola, with flashlight in her hand, walks onto the empty stage from her dressing room. Finding herself alone, she reflects on her age and her acting career.

Lola:

Gone. All gone. This is a fine joke. I must have fallen asleep in my dressing room when the play was over, and there I was gently dreaming after everyone else has left the theatre. Ah, I'm a foolish old woman, a poor, lonely creature. I shouldn't have drunk that champagne. It always makes me sleepy. And a little fat. What a fool am I, what a bloody fool. *(Calls aloud.)* George. Edgar. Eddie. Where the devil are you?

They've gone. They've left me. Alone. Alone. All, all alone. *(Looks around suspiciously.)* There's not a sound. They've all gone. I gave them my car to go to the party and they've gone without me. They've probably locked up the theatre and I shall die here.

(In Lady Macbeth pose, she holds the flashlight pointing to her face.) "Out, damned spot." *(Turns off the flashlight and holds it in front of her like a candle.)* "Out, I say. One, two. Why, then,

'tis time to do it. Hell is murky. Fie, my lord, fie, a soldier and afraid? What need we fear who knows it, when none can call our power to account? Yet who would have thought the old man to have so much blood in him." *(Sits down in the rocking chair again quietly, then rocks back and forth furiously.)* "A horse! A horse! My kingdom for a horse." *(Stops abruptly.)* I was a fool to take this tour. "You've got to make America love you again," that fool agent told me. "Look at Bette Davis. Look at Joan Crawford," he told me. *(Stands up and looks from her feet up.)* Well, look at me. I've drunk too much champagne. *(Feeling her face.)* Good heavens, my body is burning all over. I've got twenty tongues in my mouth. It's horrid. It's idiotic. This was to be my chance for a comeback. And here I am, alone, deserted, and I don't even know what I'm doing here.

(Goes to stool and leans on it.) My head is splitting. I am shivering all over. I feel as dark and cold as if I were in a cellar. Even if I don't care about my health, I should have remembered my figure. Flo Ziegfeld himself told me my figure was my fortune. *(Examining her hips.)* It has expanded. I wonder if my banker knows. And at my age, too. I'll never get my figure back. At my age I should know better. I'm sixty... I'm almost sixty. Well, at least I'm past fifty. I must admit that. One cannot be a star with Barrymore, with Leslie Howard, with... what were their names? Where have they gone? I'm old. Face it, Lola, you are old and you are a fool.

(Goes back to rocking chair, sits huddled.) The time has come for me to play a mummy, whether I like it or not. It's strange... but I feel... I feel death here on this stage. I've been an actress for forty-five years and for the first time I feel as though I'm playing a walk-on for death. *(Rises and walks slowly.)* How

dark it is here. I can't see a thing. The wind blows through this empty theatre like a train in a midnight subway. What a place for ghosts. George! Eddie! Edgar! Where the devil are you all? The shivers are running down my back. What on earth makes me think of such things? I must give up drinking. I must exercise. And no more rich foods. I'm an old woman. I won't live much longer. At my age, people go to church and prepare for death. Here I am, an old fool, still playing at games on a miserable stage. And look at me. I'm a fright. I must get out of here. I shall die of fright.

(Starts offstage, sees Hedda.) Who are you? What do you want? You're death and you've come to take me.

◆◆◆

Lola [2]
58 years old

About the scene: Lola speaks to the cleaning woman, Hedda, reflecting on a difficult choice from her past that put romantic love and a normal life at odds with her love of acting.

Lola:

My audience has gone home. They are all asleep, and I have been forgotten. They have forgotten their make-believe queen. I am as dead as Essex. No, nobody needs me, nobody loves me. I have no husband, no children. But I am still a woman. I am still alive. Warm, red blood is tingling in my veins, the blood of noble ancestors. I am an aristocrat, Hedda. I am really an aristocrat. It was not just publicity. In these veins flows the blood of the conquerors of California. And I was beautiful once, and desirable. But now look at me. What has become of the old days? There's the pit that has swallowed them all! I remember it all now. Forty-five years of my life lie buried here on this stage, and what a life, Hedda. What a life! I can see it as clearly as I see your face... the ecstasy of youth, passion, the crowds, the love of men... men, Hedda! [...]

You should have lived, Hedda, as I lived. When I first went on the stage, in the first glow of passionate youth, I remember a young man who loved me for my acting. He was beautiful, graceful as a poplar, young, shy, pure, and radiant as a summer dawn. His smile would charm away the darkest night. I remember I stood before him once, as I am now standing before you. He had never seemed so handsome to me as he did then. He wanted me to marry him. He would have given me everything. He was rich, the heir to one of the largest fortunes in America. But he wanted me to give up the stage. Give up the stage, do you understand? He could love an actress, but marry her? Never. I was in a play that day, a happy play by Noel Coward... I'll Leave It to You, I think. The play was a failure but Noel was wonderful and I was happy to give him his start. But my lover, he wanted me to give up the stage. I sent him away and the next week I was doing Roxane in Cyrano. Then, right in the middle of the last scene, I felt my eyes being opened. I saw that the worship of my art that I had held so sacred was a delusion, an empty dream. I knew at that moment that I was a fool, the plaything of the idleness of strangers. I understood my audience, my fans, at last. I have not, since that day, believed in their applause, their cheers, their expressions of love. They don't know me. Not the real me. I am as the dirt beneath their feet. They want to meet me, to hold my band, to get my autograph.

But they think all actresses are monsters, and they feel sorry for any friend who marries one of us. I have no faith in them, no faith in them at all. I saw through it all that day, Hedda. After that I wandered aimlessly about, living from day to day without looking ahead. I took parts that had no art in them—cardboard figures of tinsel. I had done all the great parts... Cleopatra, Joan, Nora, Juliet. I had been a great artist once, but little by little I threw away my talent. I gave Hollywood my throat and they choked the life out of me. I, who had played with Barrymore, had become the plaything of the Marx brothers, the girl back home for Gary Cooper, the other woman in a Warner Baxter triangle. I lost the power to express myself. I lost my looks. I lost my figure. I have been swallowed up in that great black pit. I never felt it before, but tonight when I woke up I looked back, and there behind me lay fifty-eight... almost sixty years. I have just found out what it is to be old. It is all over. *(Sobs.)* All over.

The Last Leaf

Adapted by Thomas Hischak

About the play: The bittersweet O. Henry adaptation involves Johnsy, a young artist, who lives with her friend Sue in an artists' colony in Greenwich Village, New York City. Johnsy is suffering from a severe case of pneumonia and has lost her will to live. A friend provides the ultimate gift to Johnsy, but in doing so, sacrifices his own life to save hers.

Time period: 1907.

Sue
20s

About the scene: The critically ill Johnsy has just told Sue that as the leaves fall off the ivy vine one by one, Johnsy will get more and more ill until the last leaf falls… and she dies. There are only six leaves left on the tree now, and Johnsy is afraid she'll die soon. Sue chastises Johnsy for believing such nonsense, even though the doctor had just warned Sue that Johnsy's odds for recovering were only one in ten.

Sue:

Oh, I've never heard such nonsense! What have old ivy leaves to do with your getting well? And you used to love that vine so, you naughty girl! Don't be such a goose. Why, the doctor told me that your chances for getting well real soon were—let's see exactly what he said: he said the chances were ten to one! Why, that's almost as good a chance as we have in New York when we ride on the street cars or walk past a new building. Try to take some broth now and let Susie go back to her drawing, so she can sell it to the editor. Then I'll buy port wine for you and pork chops for my greedy self.

(Sits on edge of bed, blocking the window.) Johnsy, dear, will you promise me to keep your eyes closed and not look out the window until I'm done working? I must hand those drawings in by tomorrow. I need the light, or I would draw the shade down. Just try to sleep, dear. Please...?

Life Is Like a Double Cheeseburger

By Flip Kobler and Finn Kobler

About the play: A compilation of individual scenes and monologues all loosely centered around this delicious metaphor meant to represent the many layers of human existence, this play is comedic and contemplative, healing and heartbreaking. We meet families, couples, friends, and waitstaff facing major life changes, following—or failing to follow—their dreams, and gulping down helpings of humor and humility along with their life lessons.

Time period: The present.

Amy
20s

About the scene: On a first date with Clark, Amy gets in her head and reads way too much into every little detail.

Amy:

He knows it's my favorite. I think he likes me. *(Beat.)* Wait… how did he know? Has he been stalking me? *(To Clark.)* How did you know it was my favorite? […]

(To audience.) He asked my best friend. I think he likes me. But why was he talking to Veronica? Does he want to ask Veronica out? […]

He wanted to ask me out for, like, months. He must really, really like me! Wait. Why was he nervous to ask me out? *(To Clark.)* Why were you nervous? Am I intimidating or something? […]

(To audience.) He doesn't find me intimidating? What's up with that? *(To Clark.)* You think I'm weak? You think I'm some kind of pushover? Some kind of harpy, then?

(To audience.) He's looking at his texts? Who'd be texting him now? Unless it's his buddies, checking up on how the date's going. He must really... But look at his face. He's not smiling. Why is he so serious? Am I not fun? Did he just say I'm not fun? Maybe it's not his friends. Maybe it's his ex-girlfriend. They broke up, like, three months ago. Maybe that's the three-month thing where he was trying to work it out with her and couldn't and moved on to his second choice. Well, nobody calls me "second choice." What if I'm not second choice? What if he only went out with me to make her jealous? Then I'm just a pawn. A tool. *(Clark laughs lightly and sends a text.)*

He's laughing now? It's a secret joke? I'm just some sort of secret joke? I don't have to sit here and listen to this! Forget it, I never liked him that much anyway. *(Gets up and storms off.)*

Carla
40s

About the scene: After serving some of her regular customers, Carla, who has waitressed at the same diner for more than twenty years, reminisces about why she loves the place.

Carla:

Why do I work at a diner? I know everyone, and it's close to home. Boom! Easiest answer I've ever given. *(Smiles.)* I got hired here in high school. "Go Tritons!" And it helped put me through college. You wouldn't expect kitchen grease and leather booths to clear up acne or student loans, but hey, you'd be surprised. After I graduated college, my friends encouraged me to travel more, go places. But the bug never really bit me.

My dad was a photojournalist. He went everywhere, but the sights and culture of fifty-two different countries didn't seem to stop him from cheating on my mom. Or my stepmom. Or my second stepmom. He was a nomad, constantly moving. That's one of the things about movement, though—it gives me motion sickness. My dad was just the opposite. He walked a few righteous paths, but that's when he got queasy and left unsatisfied.

Life's a journey, that's what they say. Whoever "they" are, that mysterious "they" who seem to know everything and judge everyone. Like a middle-aged waitress scavenging tips in a diner at the bottom of an off-ramp in a small, New England town. Do "they" know that half our business is travelers whose lives dance with mine in a forty-five-minute waltz? I hear their tales of great adventures beyond the horizon. Stories of exotic lands and opportunities that don't involve grease and mops and fluorescent lights. And while those sirens may call, they do not convince. A forty-five minute dance leads to... well... motion sickness.

And let me just say, my husband and I have been together twenty-two years, nausea-free. I can't say this place is entirely responsible for that, but the other half of my clientele is locals whose lives sing with mine in a never-ending symphony. Who wants to let their shoes do the talking when you've got voices like theirs? I know these people's voices by heart—their names, their stories, and their "usuals." Phil's got a rasp and always asks for his steak rare. They'd moo if he had his way. I love the way Carl looks at his wife from across the booth, even though his eyesight has been shabby these past few years or, well, decades. I remember when his hair was neither salt nor pepper, but a healthy harvest of seasoning-free locks. Like, not even garlic. I'm serious.

And I love the Sunday morning crowd. I love my ten-year-old apron. I love how a banana cream pie may not heal a broken heart, but it can dry a few tears. And if you don't agree, you haven't eaten enough banana cream pie. Here, I'm healthy. Health to me is being part of countless prom nights, promotions, birthdays, graduations, and even deaths. Let the horizon beckon. The fulfilled soreness of my feet after a day's work cantillates right back. The wattage of my smile has enough electricity to power a dozen trans-Atlantic airplanes. Granted, I think they use fossil fuels, but you get the point. People who travel everywhere are wanderers, still trying to figure out what they want. Me? I'm already here.

◆◆◆

Liz
27 years old

About the scene: During her very first speed date with a man named Donald, Liz is over-amped, nervous, and guarded. She's dammed up her emotions, and they finally spill out.

Liz:

Hi. I'm Liz. Kind of new to this whole speed-dating thing. Feels a little unnatural. I mean, how much can you learn about a person in ten minutes? Right? What does that give us, five minutes each to tell our life story? The website says "ten minutes will change your life." I seriously doubt it! But you've got to be in it to win it, right?

So... should I start? Tell you about me and then you tell me about you and then we meet in the middle somewhere and talk about our favorite movies and books and feel a little better about ourselves until we both go home alone? Hey, I think I'm starting to understand how this works!

Okay. My name is Liz. I live uptown at— Ha! On second thought, I'm not going to tell you exactly where I live in case you're an escaped mental patient or something. Let's see... I'm an actuary for an insurance company. Actuary! That's a ten-dollar name for a two-bit job. I'm an accountant. Since college. *(Groans.)* Yes, I sit in a cubicle all day and crunch numbers under fluorescent light. It's a good job, I guess. It's just not what I dreamed I'd be doing when I left Dartmouth five years ago.

I'm twenty-seven. Twenty-seven—geez! I've been a bridesmaid four times this year. Four. 'Cause all my friends seem to be getting married. But not me. Mr. Right or Prince Charming or whoever aren't into insurance actuaries, apparently. Maybe it's cubicles—I don't know. Or maybe it's me. Probably me. But my parents told me, "Liz, you need to try something different." So... here I am looking for Mr. Charming in ten-minute blocks.

Sorry. I'm venting or rambling or something-ing. I don't know. What about you? Tell me about you.

Little Women

Adapted by Gary Peterson

About the play: This fine adaptation of the literary classic by Louisa May Alcott is rich with strong and superb acting roles for all performers. Four sisters, each with a distinctively different personality, offer an irresistible charm as we see them grow up to experience life's joys and disappointments. Gary Peterson has much experience adapting classics for the stage, and here he has deftly selected many of the most charming and memorable scenes from the story to dramatize the magic that makes the book such an enduring classic. This staging radiates the timeless essence of a family that cares deeply for one another—the inspiration and pathos, the laughter and love.

Time period: 1860s

Amy
Teens

About the scene: Amy is the youngest and most pampered of the March sisters. Jo and Meg have left her home alone while they have gone out to the theatre with some boys; Beth is babysitting the Hummel's children. Amy is beyond herself with frustration and anger, wishing she was asked out to a night at the theatre instead of her sisters. In retaliation, she burns Jo's manuscript in the fireplace—a book that holds every single piece of Jo's writings.

Amy:

Leave me all alone will they? Beth has gone over to the Hummel house. "Just for a minute," she says, "Just for a minute!" And Jo and Meg! Off to the theatre! Off to the theatre with those boys! Oh, I did so want to see that play. "You can go next week with Beth!" Meg says. "Laurie only got four tickets!" Jo says. Oh, I bet it is just the nicest play. I wanted to go. Jo could have stayed home and she could go next week with Beth. How about that? Then there would only be four people. That's what they should have done. Take me, not take prissy Meg or stuck-up Jo. Well, I'll show them! Things could happen when I'm home alone. Anything could happen.

(Her eyes light on Jo's beloved manuscript, lying on top of the writing desk. She looks at it, looks away and again and then glances at their fireplace. Suddenly, impulsively, she grabs the manuscript and throws it into the fireplace.)

That'll teach 'em! That'll teach Jo!

(She is rocking back and forth, looking at the fireplace. Suddenly she is regretful, and grabs for the fire tongs. At that instant, a door opens. Startled, she dives onto the divan, covers herself over with a blanket, and pretends to be asleep.)

Jo
Late teens - early 20s

About the scene: Jo has gone away to boarding school in New York to work on her writing. Here, she writes a letter home to her mother and sister Beth. Her letter centers on describing a peculiar tutor she has met at the boarding house—his name is Professor Bhaer, and he teaches German and English to the students.

Jo:

Dear Marmee and Beth, Now that I have quite settled down at Mrs. Kirke's boarding house, I thought I would take some time out for a long letter describing my life here. Mrs. Kirke welcomed me so kindly that I felt at home at once, even in this big house full of strangers. She gave me a funny little sky-parlor—an attic room really—but there is a stove in it and a nice table in a sunny window, so I can sit here and write whenever I like. There are a number of boarders here, and I want to tell you about one of them. The day I first met him, I heard one of the children—the little one, Tina—running through the house, yelling, "I want my bear, I want my bear!"

Suddenly, behind her, this funny man came crawling playfully with a bear's costume on! You see, they were playing at menagerie, and he was her pet bear.

This is particularly funny as this man's last name is also Bhaer. It seems he was a famous literature professor in Berlin but is poor as a church-mouse here in America. He is intelligent, but he is quite helpless in domestic matters. I even had to sew a button on his waistcoat one day, because he didn't know how to do it himself.

He's very good with children, and guess what? He tells me he has a friend in the publishing business, and that he will introduce me to him someday. Isn't that wonderful? Not that I'm doing bad with my writing. I've sold a number of my stories to the weekly magazines. Still, I would like to write a novel.

Oh, I've started taking German lessons from the professor on off evenings. He always says, "Yah, I teach English to the Germans, and German to the Americans. So my life is in balance." He's very witty like that. He's been very nice to me, and he is my first true friend here in New York.

Love at First Thought

By Shawn Deal

About the play: Norm has a quirky habit of sharing his favorite books by leaving them for someone else to find and hopefully treasure. When he watches a girl he's gone to school with for years, Jolaine, discover his favorite Shakespeare play he left on a park bench, they share a look and a smile that creates a magical moment of connection. Both Norm and Jolaine are with their best friends, providing the audience four different points of view on this burgeoning relationship. These perspectives are cleverly revealed through internal monologues during which the four characters speak their inner thoughts out loud.

Time period: The present

Jolaine
Late teens - early 20s

About the scene: After some initial conversation with Norm about his favorite book, Jolaine's friend Diane mentions that Norm is cute. Jolaine surprises herself by agreeing.

Jolaine:

(Looks to Diane and scoffs, then looks to Norm for a moment before returning her gaze to Diane.) He is kind of cute, isn't he? *(To herself.)* Wait a minute! When did he become cute?! Oh, I hate this! He wasn't cute yesterday! Ahhh—! *(Exasperated.)* Seriously, I didn't think he was cute yesterday or the day before that or even the day before that. What, did he wake up cute today, all of a sudden? That can't happen! If he is cute today, logic dictates, he should have been cute yesterday. And yet, I didn't notice he was cute yesterday but did notice today. My mind is playing tricks on me! It's like some sort of bomb has gone off in my head. It's sent shockwaves through my mind,

changing the way I look at him. How could it do that?! The only thing I can seemingly think about now is how cute Norm is. And I really don't want to think about that. But it's all my mind is focusing on. My mind has betrayed me! It's never betrayed me before. But I can't force this thought out of me. And, wait…! What is it doing to my body? *(Feels pulse.)* My heart is beating faster. *(Feels forehead.)* I feel a bit warmer! What is my mind doing to me? It has hijacked my entire body! This is no fair!

Mayfair Lady

Adapted by Gary Peterson

About the play: In this fresh adaptation of Shaw's Pygmalion, as cockney-speaking flower girl Eliza Doolittle transforms into a young lady under the tutelage of Professor Higgins and Colonel Pickering, she grows not just intellectually but also emotionally, developing her own personality and pride.

Time period: 1912.

Eliza
20s

About the scene: After her tutelage, Eliza leaves Professor Higgins's care due to his poor treatment of her. She finds temporary refuge at the home of his mother. Higgins shows up to seek his mother's counsel and learns that Eliza is there. Almost immediately upon her coming downstairs, Higgins begins another row, but Eliza stands her ground.

Eliza:

Oh, perhaps you did give me the words and how to pronounce them, but all the ideas in my mind behind those words are my own. As for the manners? I learned those from Colonel Pickering. While you always treated me like dirt, he always treated me like a lady. He was courteous and cordial with me from that very first day, calling me Miss Doolittle and offering me a seat. There were a hundred little things that came naturally to him that show respect to another human being. That was the beginning of my own self-respect. You see, the real difference between a lady and a flower girl is not how she behaves, but how she's treated. I shall always be a flower girl to you, because that's how you treat me and always will. But I know I can be a lady because Colonel Pickering always treated me as a lady. [...]

It's not just the manners, it's that I won't be passed over. Ignored and taken for granted. I want a little kindness. I know I'm just a common ignorant girl, and you are a book-learned gentleman— but I'm not dirt under your feet. What I did was not for the dresses and the taxis, I did it because we were pleasant together and I came to care for you. You have a good side, a gentle side— but you conceal it under bluster and boasting. *(Firm.)* Still, I can do without you. Don't think I can't.

Memory Garden

By Mark Scharf

About the play: Angie, a young widow with two young daughters devotes herself to maintaining the roadside memorial for her husband, who died in a tragic hit-and-run car accident. Angie has become such a familiar figure at the site that neighbors beep their horns and wave hello as they pass. When Dan, claiming to be a reporter, stops to get her story, Angie unexpectedly finds the answers to her own questions about what happened on that terrible day.

Time period: The present.

◆◆◆

Angie [1]
35 years old

About the scene: Angie, alone, stands directly in front of the cross at the location where her husband was killed, telling him just how much she misses him.

Angie:

I brought you a piece of my birthday cake, baby. I know how much you love birthday cake and candles. Remember when we used to make love by candlelight? When we blew out the candles you always said you loved the smell because it reminded you of blowing out the candles on a birthday cake.

It is a good smell. It always reminds me of you. Hell, everything reminds me of you.

I'm 35 years old now. Can you believe it? Thirty-five. How am I gonna live another 30 or 40 years without you?

I know, I know. I just will. I have to for the kids. And for me. And for you. I wish you could have seen what our girls did for me. Little Arlene baked the cake for me. I'd like to think you did see it all. Somehow I think you did. I feel you around me every day, baby, and I miss you so. I miss you with every cell in my body, every thought in my head—I ache for you. I don't think that ache will ever go away. I never thought I could take it, that I could live with this pain, but I do. *(Takes the watering can and waters each of the flowers in the flower pots carefully.)* The girls still won't come here. They won't come with me to your grave either. I don't make them. I don't think you're in the cemetery anyway. But somehow I feel you're here—somehow I can always sense you here so very strongly. *(Car drives by, beeps horn. She waves after the car.)* Oh, that's the Campbells. They always let me know when they drive by and see me. They've been very kind. Everyone's been very kind since you... since you went away. Now then... Let's neaten this place up a bit. *(Starts "clipping" grass and weeds around the site.)* I... have... given... up... on... killing these weeds—but I can surely keep them from growing up over everything.

Angie [2]
35 years old

About the scene: Angie tells Dan that she can still feel the presence of her deceased husband and knows that he is there because of the dragonflies.

Angie:

Sometimes it's just a feeling. Or maybe I'll be talking to him and the wind will pick up and move the wind chimes he bought me. Or a candle will flicker. Or sometimes I'm driving and feeling real low and be talking to him and right then the radio will play some song we both loved. And then... there are the dragonflies. They show up at times when Steve would've been there. Like one time, my oldest girl won a ribbon at a swim meet. And we were driving home, and she was sayin' how she wished her daddy could have seen her. And I was telling her that he did see her, he was there—and this dragonfly landed right on the hood of my car. I pulled the car over and stopped, and it sat there a long time. And I knew. Sometimes I'll be in the kitchen washing dishes and staring out the window wondering where in the hell I'm going to get the money to pay for this or that, and I'll look up and there'll be a dragonfly hovering right outside the window looking at me. [...]

No... I told you I'm not crazy.

But I think he sends them. To let me know he's still here.

The Mirror of Dori Gray

By John Mattera

About the play: The essence of Oscar Wilde's haunting tale, *The Picture of Dorian Gray*, is captured in this unique, modern-day view. Years have passed since Dori watched an old woman die outside the school library. This old woman, however, was actually Sarah, a girl in Dori's high school. Dori took Sarah's backpack as a cruel joke, but inside the backpack was a mirror that kept Sarah young and alive. As long as Dori has the mirror with her, she, too, will remain young and beautiful. Like Wilde intended in the original story, Dori's vanity causes her to become misguided and lost, snared in a web… a trap which even abducts her best friend Samantha.

Time period: The present.

◆◆◆

Dori
16 - 18

About the scene: Dori has just had a nightmare that her mirror is gone and the cops have discovered the truth about her past murders. In her dream, Dori, now old and ugly without her mirror, tries to talk her way out of arrest.

Dori:

All right! So what?! How am I supposed to act now, like a rabbit snared by the likes of two Keystone cops? I don't think so. What does it prove that I said "mirror" and you didn't? A pall of virulent gossip has tried to choke the breath from me, has robbed me of my best years. Relentless hounds have nipped at my heels, forced me into seclusion like some monastic fanatic… no, like some outcast leper. Fear, hate, the depravity of human nature has fueled my defamation. The hypocrites have descended vulture-like upon me, fooling themselves, spewing their foul hypocrisies. They're the ones who should gaze at their true reflections instead of professing their transparent piety. They're the ones who should listen to their consciences, repent for their own sins, instead of fabricating diversions, spinning monstrous scandals about me. I know what they say about me. *(Mimics.)* "She got so ugly because they stole her mirror. Mirror, mirror on the wall, who's the fairest of them all? Not Dori Gray. Oh, no, not anymore. Not since we snatched her mirror." I've heard it all, and I'm weary. *(Snarls.)* So, what is it you want? If you'd come to arrest me, you would have done it by now. You've got nothing on me. Nothing of any substance.

◆◆◆

Samantha
Mid - late 30s

About the scene: Samantha still does not know Dori's secret, even though they've remained friends for twenty years. Samantha confesses to Dori just how jealous she is of her.

Samantha:

Dori, considering all you've done, I don't see what you have to complain about. Life has treated you well. [...]

Yeah, it has. You haven't aged a day, haven't put on a pound, an ounce, since we were kids. You're just as beautiful now as you were then. And look at me. *(Dori starts to speak.)* Don't. Don't lie to me, trying to make me feel better. I know what I look like. I'm gross. Sometimes I feel like showering with my clothes on so I don't have to see myself. You, you're beautiful beyond words. A successful columnist practically right out of college. Men lust after you. You can pick and choose among the flock, any time you like. Me, I'm divorced. I'm lonely. I've actually toyed with putting in one of those singles ads saying, "Full-figured lonely woman with great personality seeks gentleman, 35 to 45, for possible relationship." *(An afterthought.)* "But let's do dinner first. I know every restaurant in town."

The Most Viewed Least Watched Talk Show in History

By Kenneth R. Preuss

About the play: Public-access talk show hosts Brighton and Avery don't have very good guests. Or many regular viewers. Their show, "Monumental Achievements," features anything but, as guest after guest proves to be entirely unexceptional in almost every way. But just as the hosts are about to call it a wrap on another unremarkable show, a special, last-minute guest provides a future perspective that has Brighton and Avery reconsidering everything and wondering if their show might truly wind up being the most viewed someday, even if it is the least watched talk show in history.

Time period: The present.

Quinn
20s

About the scene: One of the talk show guests, Quinn, tells the tale of her monumental achievement with a talking duck.

Quinn:

He's a duck. I named him MacDuck. [...]

It's actually a pun on the name "MacDuff" from the Scottish play. I was reading Shakespeare aloud in the woods when I started to hear my words come back to me. First, I thought it was an echo, but I noticed some ducks across the pond and figured one of them was communicating with me. I decided to call the talking duck over, so I shouted, "Duck!" All the people swimming in the pond went like this. *(Dips quickly, throws hands up defensively, and cowers.)* ...because all the ducks flew over to me, thinking I was calling them. [...]

None of them were talking at first, so I read Shakespeare as I walked along a path, and MacDuck was the only one who followed. Deep in the woods, we set up camp, and we delved into the Bard. We stayed up all night. I recited lines, and MacDuck repeated them. We recited "to be or not to be," "friends, Romans, countrymen," "fair is foul and foul is fair." We really chuckled about that one. You know, since ducks are fowl. It was a transcendent night. But things took a sad turn in the morning. [...]

I got a little... Ambitious. *(Sighs.)* Shakespeare elevates language and explores relevant themes, but everyone knows the greatest form of theatrical expression is... musical theatre. But it didn't go as planned. "Let's start with Chicago," I said, and MacDuck moved away a bit. I figured he didn't like Bob Fosse, so I suggested we shift to Oklahoma. He moved away even further. MacDuck obviously thought Chicago and Oklahoma were locations that I was suggesting he migrate to. Thank goodness I didn't say South Pacific. *(Builds up dramatically.)* I tried to think of a musical with a non-location title, but made a poor choice in shouting... Cats! Anyway, he flew to the top of a tree. I panicked and called out the most innocuous musical I could think of... Bye Bye Birdie! *(Softly and sadly.)* And MacDuck, thinking I was bidding farewell, shed a tear... lifted a wing to wave... and flew off, never to be seen again.

The Ninth Train

By Jane Jeffries and Jim Jeffries

About the play: Just before the start of World War II, Nicholas Winton organized trains to transport Jewish children out of Czechoslovakia to England. Known as the kindertransports, these trains successfully rescued 664 Jewish children. During this tragic time in history, some Jewish families had to make a grievous choice: should they separate the family and send their children away on one of these trains to safety, knowing that they may never see them again? Or do they keep the family together in Czechoslovakia and risk ultimate peril against the swiftly advancing forces of their greatest enemy? This powerful one-act drama explores one family's experiences with the growing tensions in the region and the difficult choice they have to make in hope that at least part of their family might survive.

Time period: 1939.

◆◆◆

Analise
18 years old

About the scene: Analise notices that her younger sister, Eva, is secretly reading a handwritten note behind the book she has in her hands. Analise also thought it was unusual that when she went to the bakery, Marek, the boy at the bakery, gave her an extra roll in a bag and asked her to share it with Eva. Analise puts the two together and warns Eva that their parents wouldn't approve of Eva's relationship with Marek, who is Christian. Young and naïve, Eva has not yet realized it could be dangerous for both of their families.

Analise:

That must be a very interesting book. I notice that every time you go to the bakery, your book becomes much more interesting. I mean, what could possibly be the connection between great works of literature and pumpernickel? I've always wondered.

That's why I went to the bakery today. All I bought was one little roll, as a sort of experiment, to see if my appreciation for Shakespeare would increase with each nibble. Sadly, it was not so. But it is interesting that the baker's son—I think his name is Marek? Yes, Marek gave me this special paper sack for one little roll. And he specifically asked me to share with my sister. And, lo and behold, there were two rolls in the sack. *(Pulls a small paper sack from a pocket and shakes it.)* It must be something besides bread that whets your appetite for reading. *(Serious.)* Eva, I've warned you about Marek. You know we shouldn't go sneaking around. What if Mama and Papa find out?

Edna
30s - 40s

About the scene: Edna Friedman visits her neighbor Hanna one afternoon while Hanna's children are away. Edna has heard that Nazis are forcing Jewish families in a nearby town out of their homes, and she has come to warn Hanna that they might be next. She suggests that they both register their children with the kindertransport that leaves for Britain.

Edna:

I came because I have news.

They are making the Jews in Liberec move. They were given three hours to pack and then forced to leave their homes. Ruza told me. We've had no luck at the embassies, either. I'm starting to wonder…

Have you heard of Mr. Winton? He's British. He's set up an office at a hotel in Wenceslas Square. Gitta Berkovits told me about him. He's trying to help the Jewish children. He's organizing trains to take children to Britain. British families will take care of them there. The Gentile families will keep the children safe until their parents can join them. They'll be safe from Hitler. It's unthinkable, really. But our options get fewer by the day. *(Gets an idea.)* Perhaps if we sent them together! Otto and Pavel could watch out for Rachel and Eva. Think about it, Hanna. Maybe we should get on the list just in case.

I've got to go. I'll talk to you soon.

◆◆◆

Ruza
30s - 40s

About the scene: Ruza Havel, Marek's mother and a Christian woman, visits the home of a Jewish family, Hanna and Petr Stern and their three children. She has arranged a way to save two of the Stern children from the invading Nazi soldiers, if the Sterns can act quickly, but she has no way to save their oldest child.

Ruza:

You must be quiet! *(Moves to the window to look out.)* Marek is no Nazi.

But he is stupid. I told my son to stay away from Eva. I was trying to protect her. And you. And your family. My son disobeyed me and came to see Eva last night. But it won't be long before they find out that he lied when he said Zelenka was his uncle. But now he's put your family in danger. We have friends who are trying to help... to get your people out. Which is why we've come. We've come to talk to you about Eva and Otto.

Have you heard of Nicholas Winton, the man organizing the kindertransports? We can get them out on the next train. You probably know that the Friedmans have disappeared. I'm afraid I don't know where they are. I'm sorry.

But they had two places on the next kindertransport. I contacted my friends and put Eva and Otto in their places. The train leaves today. In three hours. To Holland. Then a ship will take them to England. Families will be at the dock to take the children.

I'm sorry. Analise is too old. But your other two could still go, and we could get Otto and Eva to safety.

You have every reason not to trust us. Still, Marek insisted we come here. Honestly, I was afraid to get involved.

Marek is stupid when it comes to your daughter, but he is right. Time has run out. We're trying to help now.

Nobody Heard Me Cry

By Vern Harden

About the play: The heart and soul of a teenage boy caught in a downward spiral of depression is painfully revealed in this one-act drama. The play chronicles Justin's slow and painful deterioration through his journal entries. We learn of his anger surrounding his father's untimely death, his disappointment at not getting into the police academy, and his constant sense of isolation, even when around other kids his age. Though Justin's mother and friends try to reach out to him, he pushes them all away. Sadly, they give up too easily, not fathoming the depth of his anguish.

Time period: The present.

Mary
40s

About the scene: Justin's mother, Mary, has just told him that they'll be moving because she's going to get remarried to her friend Harold. Angry and more anguished than ever, Justin says goodbye to his mother and Harold and leaves the room, dropping his journal as he exits. In the climactic final moment of the show, Mary reads the journal and realizes the depths and source of his pain… at the very moment he commits suicide.

Mary:

(Hurries over and retrieves journal.) Justin, you dropped your journal. […]

(Opens journal.) I want to see what he's been writing. Maybe, if I could understand his feelings better. Here, at the end: "I have nothing left to give this life. And nothing left to lose. First, my father left me. Then they took away the academy. Now they want to take away my friends. My home. Last night, I did something I haven't done since I was ten years old. I went up to

my room, crawled under the covers, curled up into a ball and... cried. Today, for a while, I thought maybe I could see light at the end of the tunnel, my endless tunnel of night-black pain. But somebody turned out that light, just like they always do. And now there is nothing left."

Oh, Harold, this is so sad. He must think the whole world is against him. I thought... that my love, a mother's love would be enough. It is for most people. When did I let him down, Harold? Where have I failed him?

(Goes back to reading journal.) "I think I finally knew last night that there was only one way to make the hurting stop. I knew when I was there, in my bed... and nobody came to help. I guess the worst part about my whole life is that no matter what I said, or what I did... nobody heard me cry." *(Lowers journal slowly and bows her head.)*

Pandora's Backpack

By Laurie Bryant

About the play: The premise of the play is simple; its exploration of xenophobia is not. The play examines the varied responses by high school students to an unattended backpack at a public park. While some sequences may seem to take a lighthearted approach to the subject, there is an intentional undercurrent of discomfort. The intent is to illuminate how one misplaced object can bring out the best—and the worst—in us.

Time period: The present.

◆◆◆

Liz
16 - 18

About the scene: Liz and Ryan are high school students who are going together. When the two stumble upon an unattended backpack in the park, Ryan is the voice of reason while Liz tends to jump to conclusions and is quick to judge.

Liz:

I hate them. […]

(Points at the backpack.) Them! The people who did this! The people who make us afraid, even if nobody did this. And the people like you who aren't ever afraid and just go about their lives as if nothing bad is ever going to happen. And it doesn't… until it does, and then it's always to somebody else! […]

Nothing makes sense! Being afraid of some kid's school bag doesn't make sense. *(Kicks the bench and then recoils in fright at what she has just done. She cowers, in fear of the backpack, then slowly backs away.)* […]

Okay, I… I hate not knowing who to hate. My parents knew who to hate. So did my grandparents, and my great-grandparents.

They put on uniforms and went to war against people in different uniforms. People are supposed to know which people they hate. And I know what you're thinking, that maybe we're not supposed to hate anybody, and I get that. I really do. But they never get that memo, do they? And if they ever did, we wouldn't have to worry about stupid things like backpacks or unattended packages or airplanes or neighbors who aren't what they pretend to be, would we? *(Near tears.)* I only want to know who to hate because they hate me first, and I don't know why.

Playground
By Wil Denson

About the play: *Playground* is an exploration inside the mind of a small child whose life has fallen to pieces at an early age. Jason's dad has recently left him and his mom, and fourth grade is tough. He is constantly bullied by the sixth graders on the playground. Jason attempts to keep to himself and finds comfort in his imaginary friend, Big John. Big John is a personification of the dad he wishes he still had, and although Big John does his best to cheer him up, just like his father, he also has the propensity to let Jason down.

Time period: The present.

Margaret
10 years old

About the scene: In an attempt to get Jason involved with friends on the playground, their teacher, Miss Sheffield, has put Margaret and her friends in charge of a "welcome wagon" to invite Jason to play and feel more comfortable. Jason barely looks at the girls as they talk to him and does not take up their offer to jump rope. Margaret does her best to welcome Jason, but her efforts fall on deaf ears.

Margaret:

Miss Sheffield made us the welcoming committee. My name is Margaret. She's Susan and she's Kimberly. It's our job to welcome you. *(Pauses and stands staring at Jason for some reaction. He occasionally looks up at them but says nothing.)* Welcome to Ramsdell School. We're glad you're here. We're like the Welcome Wagon. Only we don't have any gifts to give you. *(Studies him for a moment. This is not the warm rewarding charity work she had expected. She is nearly at the end of her planned welcoming remarks.)*

(Indicating Susan's jump rope.) Do you want to play jump rope with us? *(Jason does not respond.)* *Well, do you or don't you?* *(Silence.)* Well, then, do you know where everything is? Would you like us to show you anything? *(Jason stares at the ground. Margaret is losing patience.)*

(Taking out her frustration on her friends.) Well, you're supposed to say something too! *(Turning to Jason.)* Well, do—do you know where the boys' bathroom is? Would you like us to show you? *(There is a shocked pause then an eruption of scandalized giggles. Wrathfully.)* That's not funny! It's nothing to laugh at! We're supposed to be the welcoming committee and help people find where things are. That's our job. I'm just doing what we're supposed to. I'm going to tell Miss Sheffield how silly you are! *(To Jason again.)* We're going over to the swings now. There's another new boy there. He's from Texas. Do you want to come with us? *(Jason shakes his head no. Somewhat relieved.)* Well, you can come if you want to.

Pollyanna

Adapted by Susan Pargman

About the play: This is the classic tale of the greatest optimist of all time... Pollyanna. It's the story how a little girl's faith in her father's promise—that you can find something good about anything that happens—guides her steadfastly through circumstances that most adults would find formidable. Pollyanna becomes an orphan, and she is placed into the care of her purely pessimistic and domineering aunt, Miss Harrington. The town itself isn't much better. Led by a fire and brimstone pastor whose favorite Bible verse is "Woe unto you," folks are always complaining, feeling sorry for themselves, and viewing their existence as dark and dreary. Yet, Pollyanna faithfully plays her "Glad Game," innocently teaching it to others wherever she goes.

Time period: 1910.

Mrs. Payson
Late 40s - 50s

About the scene: Since the orphaned Pollyanna has no other living relatives, her aunt, Miss Harrington, has been her new guardian. Pollyanna quickly made herself at home in her new community, so when she was hit by a car and at risk of being paralyzed, it touched everyone. Mrs. Payson is one of those in town who has been greatly impacted by Pollyanna and her Glad Game. She asks Miss Harrington to give Pollyanna a message from her.

Mrs. Payson:

My name is Mrs. Payson. Mrs. Jack Payson. I presume you've heard of me. Most of the good people in this town have. And maybe some of the things you've heard ain't true. But never mind that. It's about the little girl I come. I heard about the accident, and it broke me all up. Maybe you don't know it, but I've seen a good deal of that little girl of yours. We live on the

Pendleton Hill Road, and she used to go by often. Only she didn't always go by. She came in and played with the kids and talked to me, and my man, when he was home. She seemed to like it, and to like us. She didn't know, I suspect, that her kind of folks don't generally call on my kind. Maybe if they did call more, Miss Harrington, there wouldn't be so many of my kind. Be that as it may, she came; and she didn't do herself no harm, and she did do us good. A lot o' good. How much she won't know, nor can't know, I hope. 'Cause if she did, she'd know other things that I don't want her to know.

But it's just this. It's been hard times with us this year, in more ways than one. We've been blue and discouraged, my man and me, and ready for 'most anything. We was reckoning on getting a divorce about now, and letting the kids... well, we didn't know yet what we would do with the kids. Then came the accident, and what we heard about the little girl's giving up hope and all. And we got to thinking how Pollyanna used to come and sit on our doorstep and train with the kids and laugh and just be so glad. She was always being glad about somethin' and then, one day, she told us why, and about The Game, you know; and she tried to coax us to play it. Well, we've heard now that she's fretting her poor little life out of her, because she can't play it no more... that there's nothing to be glad about. And that's what I came to tell her today. That maybe she can be a little glad for us, 'cause we've decided to stick to each other and play The Game ourselves. I know she would be glad, because she used to feel kind of bad at things we said sometimes. Just how The Game is going to help us, I can't say that I exactly see, yet. But maybe 'twill. Anyway, we're going to try, 'cause she wanted us to. Will you tell her?

◆◆◆

Pride and Prejudice

Adapted by Rebecca Gellott

About the play: This superbly written adaptation restores many popular scenes and conversations from the book that are often cut from other screen and stage adaptations. Revisit all your favorite characters here: witty, free-spirited Elizabeth Bennet and her four sisters, including the lovely Jane; Mrs. Bennet, who only wants what's best for her daughters; Mr. Bennet, who has made it his life's work to affectionately make sport of his wife; and of course, the suitors, Mr. Darcy, Charles Bingley, and George Wickham.

Time period: Early 1800s.

◆◆◆

Elizabeth
20s

About the scene: Darcy's aunt, Lady Catherine, comes to Elizabeth, demanding to know if she has accepted Darcy's hand in marriage. After much coaxing, Elizabeth declares that she refused him when he proposed, but since that time, was proven wrong in her understanding of Darcy's character. Unbeknownst to Elizabeth, Darcy is listening in.

Elizabeth:

Lady Catherine, when I was your guest at Rosings Park, Mr. Darcy called upon me at Hunsford Parsonage, and he did offer his hand. […]

I refused him. […]

I care not for Pemberley. Or Derbyshire or all the riches I know he could offer. I cared only for my own happiness, and I was convinced, Your Ladyship, he could not make me happy.

You see, your nephew slighted me at an assembly once. And I'm afraid I never forgave him for that. […]

In my wounded vanity, I chose to believe the very worst about him. I allowed myself to be entirely misled in my understanding of his character, and when every day there was evidence of his growing affection and regard for me, I chose to see only arrogance and conceit. I treated him with mockery and contempt, gave him no encouragement and still he came to Hunsford... and spoke of love.

It is many months since that I have come to realize how very wrong I had been. To bear witness to his goodness and kindness, his unfathomable generosity, his loyalty and devotion to his friends, his sister—I don't believe I have ever known a better man. And I am quite certain I could never love any other. So I cannot promise what you ask, Your Ladyship. I can only promise that if I were still so fortunate as to be loved by Mr. Darcy... there isn't a soul in the world who could induce me to refuse him now. Least of all you.

Lydia
Late teens - early 20s

About the scene: Lydia, Elizabeth's youngest sister, and Mr. Wickham have just eloped during a seemingly innocent weekend in London. Here, Lydia recounts the weekend's events to Elizabeth, who is not keen on hearing the details. Mr. Wickham had previously slighted Elizabeth, lying about his debts and manipulating her into liking him. Lydia is ecstatic about the wedding, recalling how Darcy saved the day and paid for the ceremony to happen, and in her excitement reveals information meant to remain secret.

Lydia:

Lizzy! Why have you not joined us? You have missed my account of our wedding! Are you not curious about the affair? [...]

(Giggles and hitches on to her arm.) You are so strange. But I must tell you how it went off. We were married, you know, at St. Clement's. And it was all settled that we should be there by eleven o'clock! My uncle and I went together—and the others were to meet us by the church. Well, Monday morning came, and I was in such a fuss! And then I should have gone quite distracted... […]

When he was late, I started to worry that the groomsman might never show! But luckily, I remembered that even if he'd been prevented, the wedding need not be delayed. We had an able substitute in Mr. Darcy! […]

Why, of course! It was Mr. Darcy who discovered us in London. He brought Wickham to the church! Well, someone had to pay for the vicar and the flowers, Lizzy! Not to mention Wickham's debts in London that needed settling and all his creditors back in Brighton before we— *(Gasps, suddenly horrified.)* Oh, gracious me! I quite forgot! […]

I ought not to have said a word! It was to be such a secret! I promised Mr. Darcy so faithfully. He was adamant that no one must know! Oh. *(Glances toward her "dear" Wickham.)* What will Wickham say?

Purple Ink

By B.G. Craig

About the play: Diane Fletcher is dead, but her story is not over. Diane's estranged daughters, Kay and Melody, have arrived to clean out their childhood home but are shocked to learn their mother had become a hoarder in her final years. As they clean up the mess left behind, both literally and emotionally, by their mother, the sisters realize that, like the purple buffalo innocently scrawled on the wallpaper from a childhood long ago, traces from the past leave an indelible imprint on their hearts.

Time period: The present.

◆◆◆

Kay
40s

About the scene: Kay is surprised to learn that her mother was in a book club and reflects on her difficulty seeking her mother's acceptance, especially once she revealed she wanted to be a novelist. Learning now that her mother appreciated books resurfaces the pain of rejection that she had buried years earlier, and she expresses it here to her sister, aunt, and her mother's book club friends.

Kay:

You don't understand. I actually wanted to be a writer, a book author. But when I chose not to return to school so I could write my book instead, Mom cut me off. She wouldn't even read what I had written so far! Said that books wouldn't put food on the table, and that I was wasting my time. All this time, I figured she just hated reading—didn't get the appeal. But no... I come to find out, she has quite an appreciation for reading. Yes, she loves to read books—except mine!

She always goes out of her way to insult me. She's always that little voice in my head, poking and prodding and constantly telling me that I'm not good enough! I'm never good enough. I can never be enough to impress any of you. I'm a lonely, bitter woman with a low-pay, dead-end job who dropped out of college to write some 300-page piece of rejected material. My own mother cut me off, and I cut her out of my life in response. I never amounted to anything, and in her last days, Mom still probably resented my very existence. She was too ashamed of me to even mention me to her Book Club friends!

I've had it up to here with you. I've had it up to here with all of you. I don't have to stand around and feel unwelcome in my childhood home. I only came because I want the ring. Otherwise, you can burn the house down with everything in it. I just want my mother's wedding ring.

Carol
60s

About the scene: Diane's sister, Carol, is helping sort through all the piles at Diane's house. They find a book in Diane's handwriting, which Carol grabs before anyone else can see it. She tells Kay and Melody that it's just a recipe book her sister kept. Sometime later, however, Melody flips through the book and sees that it's actually her mother's diary. Pressed by her nieces about why she lied to them, Carol tries to clear the air, and in doing so, reveals the cause behind Diane's downfall and her own sense of guilt in enabling the behavior.

Carol:

Okay... okay. I'll explain myself. You won't like it, but it doesn't matter because the diary is mine now, and you begged me to tell you this...

Melody, I'm sorry I behaved the way I did. I'm just… ashamed of what this diary must say about me. Diane… she had her demons. We are all aware of this, yes? Well, in many ways, I feel like I have been an enabler for her. I… well, I knew about your mother's drinking before anyone else, but… I was in denial. Then, one night, she had so much to drink that she passed out on the couch, and she wasn't watching David, and he had really become a strong walker at that point and… Well, if I had pushed her to get help, maybe she wouldn't have passed out that night. Maybe she could've taken David to the ER in time…

That's why I didn't come to the funeral, Kay. I felt so guilty, like it was all my fault. I'm sure what Diane felt was even worse, and I think that's what began the hoarding. She never wanted to lose him, so she kept his cups, drawings, toys, clothes… Then it wasn't just his stuff anymore, it was everything. For the longest time, you girls didn't know because I let her keep things in my garage. Then my garage overflowed, so I got her a storage unit, because I knew she couldn't afford it herself. But I was just enabling her because I felt so guilty. My sister was suffering. I just wanted to help. *(Takes a deep breath.)* Diane did try to get help, though. She wanted to be better… for you both.

◆◆◆

Melody
Late 30s - early 40s

About the scene: After Kay storms out in anger, Melody is upset and calls out after her, attempting to reason with her. When her sister doesn't respond, Melody finds herself alone, talking to her dead mother while surrounded by her garbage.

Melody:

You don't talk about things, Kay! When you have an issue, you never want to actually talk about it and make it better. You did that to Mom, and now you're doing it to me again! *(Silence.)* Don't you have anything to say? *(Silence.)*

Fine, don't respond. I'll just talk to Mom! Maybe her spirit is floating around here somewhere. She'll listen to the things I have to say... Hi, Mom! It's Melody. How are you, Mom? Where have you been? I don't know whether you're in heaven or hell, but I hope you're having a blast! Either option has got to be better than staying here with your daughter. But hey, when did you ever want to spend time with me, anyways? Maybe you went and died just to make it easier to forget about your children. *(Stands indignant for a moment, then takes a seat.)*

I– I'm sorry, Mom. I get so mad sometimes, and I don't even know what I'm saying. Mark tells me all the time that our marriage would be better if I'd just shut up. *(Silence.)* I want things to be better between Kay and me... I really do.

Kay's so absorbed in herself that she never looks around her anymore! It's always about her. Her relationship troubles, her financial situation, her regrets. I feel smothered by her negativity. It's almost like if she can't beat me in successes, she has to beat me in failures. But... my life isn't perfect. My marriage to Mark? I don't know... *(Looks into the trash bag and sighs.)*

You kept everything, Mom. Grudges, secrets, junk. I mean, look at all this crap, Mom. What's the point in keeping this? What in this house is worth keeping? Worth remembering? *(Pulls a tattered manual from a box.)* Oh, here's the manual for the microwave you couldn't figure out... fifteen years ago. After three bags of burnt popcorn, you tossed the microwave, but apparently you didn't feel the need to toss the manual!

Quaran-Teens

By Laurie Allen

About the play: This play consists of 15 four- to seven-minute original monologues that explore a variety of teen responses to the pandemic and the safer-at-home restrictions that came with it. From restoring old friendships and keeping traditions alive to missing baseball, graduation, prom, and so much more, each character portrays an arc to move past their anger, disappointment, and bitterness and show the resiliency of teens. Each monologue offers a unique, true-to-life point of view of this real-world crisis that maintains an element of hope for a brighter future.

Time period: 2020.

◆◆◆

Morgan
Teens

About the scene: After a fight with her mom, Morgan calms herself down by feeding and talking to the ducks at the park.

Morgan:

(Throws a piece of bread.) I always liked feeding you. Mom would bring me to the park almost every weekend when I was a kid. At first, I was scared of you. I thought you were going to bite me. So, I'd run away and hide behind a tree. Mom would just stand there laughing and feed you while I watched. She would talk to you, too, like I'm talking to you now. But finally, I figured out you weren't going to hurt me. Maybe a little peck here or there because you got too anxious for the bread, but it never hurt. Now... this is how I relax.

(Throws bread.) Earlier, Mom and I had this big fight, and... I don't know. I guess I said some things I didn't mean. I mean... I was mean. "You can't control me! You can't force me to stay

here! I'm sick of this house! Sick of these walls! And I'm sick of you! So, I'm leaving, and you can't stop me! I'm leaving! Do you hear me? I'm leaving!"

I went to my room and slammed the door. I thought... I'm just going to grab some things... you know, pack a bag... and leave! I'll sleep in the park if I have to. What's she going to do? Call the police? Get me arrested for going to the park? *(Throws bread.)* Then, I hear this tap, tap, tap.

"Morgan, can I come in?"

"No! Go away! I'm busy!"

I wanted her to think I was packing my bag. I even opened and closed drawers to make it sound that way. I know she was standing outside listening. I felt ashamed, but yet... I wanted to leave. So, I grabbed my backpack, threw a few things inside of it and walked into the living room. Mom gave me a defeated look. I know she was tired of fighting. I was, too.

But we kind of had this stare. No words, just staring. I'm almost daring her to stop me from walking out that door and she's pleading with her eyes, "Please don't go." My independent nature is screaming, "Do it! Show her! She can't boss you around! No one can!"

Then all of a sudden, I had this vision. I saw my mom standing in the park with ducks circling her. They were quacking. She was laughing. And I was hiding behind that big elm tree. "Come on, Morgan," she said. Don't be scared! They won't hurt you."

Yeah... I hurt my mom. I could see it in her eyes. I tossed my backpack to the couch and said, "I want to go feed the ducks." She nodded and didn't say a word. Within a couple seconds, she had the car keys in one hand and a loaf of bread in the other. We didn't say one word on the drive over here. Silence. When she parked on the street, I grabbed the loaf of bread and came straight here.

(Glances back.) She's just sitting there. Waiting. I'm glad she's giving me some space. I need it. *(Throws bread.)* Because ever since I quit hiding behind that elm tree, this has been my hiding place. The park. The ducks. The memories of all those times my mom brought me here. It's comforting and makes me feel at peace. *(Throws bread.)* And now... now I feel bad. I don't like the way things are now. I want things to go back to normal. Whatever that is. But at least here, I feel normal.

(Gets a piece of bread.) Hey little one back there, are you hungry? You big guys up here are always snatching up all the food. *(Throws the bread hard.)* Here you go.

I bet you're glad you don't have to be in quarantine. I mean, you can swim all over the pond, all day long. Go wherever you want. Hang out with your friends. But I guess if you could leave this place, you wouldn't. Home is nice. Safe. Comforting. But I do miss my friends. Mom said it won't be like this forever. But there is one thing I hope never changes. Coming here. Feeding you guys. Even before I was big enough to walk, Mom would push me in the stroller to see you. Then I hid. And now, I'm not scared at all.

Okay, guys, guess I'll be going. I have some apologies to make. And don't worry. I'll be back soon.

◆◆◆

Rememberin' Stuff

By Eleanor Harder

About the play: When a group of high school drama students is given the assignment to share their memories with each other, the result is an eclectic collection of hilarious, heartfelt, serious, intense, and inspiring scenes and monologues.

Time period: The present.

Barbara
Teens

About the scene: Barbara knows how certain things can remind you of specific events—like, a particular chair reminds her of when her parents got divorced. She remembers hiding behind the chair, listening to her grandpa give advice to her mother about getting a divorce. (NOTE: As a monologue, the actor also delivers her grandpa's line.)

Barbara:

Funny how things remind you of something. I mean, like that big chair over there. *(Points down left.)* It reminds me of when I first heard that my mom and dad were going to get divorced. Oh, there'd been talk about a divorce for quite a while, so I guess I really shouldn't have been surprised. But somehow, I never thought it would happen. I suppose that's because I didn't want it to. It wasn't until I heard my mom talking to my grandfather that day that I had a pretty good idea that it was going to happen. Grandpa was an attorney, and I remember he came to our house one afternoon. It was summer, and it was hot, and I was seven. They were in the living room, talking very quietly and very seriously. I couldn't hear everything, but I heard enough to know that Grandpa was telling Mom what she should do to get a divorce from my dad. And that made me mad! It wasn't his business, it was ours! And my dad wasn't even there! He was at work. Maybe he didn't even know this was happening. And I loved my dad. And I just felt—terrible! I remember I came into the room, and I guess I said something that wasn't very nice. I don't remember what, but I remember vividly what my grandpa said.

"That's enough out of you! Can't you see we're talking? Now go away and leave us alone, you little brat!"

Nobody had ever called me a brat before. I remember I didn't say anything more, but I didn't leave, either. I couldn't leave. They were destroying my life! I remember I went over to the big upholstered armchair in the corner. It was brown. I crawled behind it to hide. *(Crouches.)* They knew I was there. It was in the same room with them, so I guess I wasn't really hiding from them especially. Just hiding from what was happening in my life. *(Sighs as she stands up.)* But it didn't matter where I was. Mom and Dad got a divorce anyway. *(Shrugs.)* I don't think about it much anymore. It was a long time ago. But I still think about that brown chair—and hiding. Because sometimes I still hide from what's happening in my life. It's almost like I'm crawling behind that stupid brown chair again. But, you know, I think most people have their own brown chairs. I don't mean they actually have brown chairs. I mean, I think most people hide their real feelings and their fears. And sometimes I think they hide who they really are. So I guess I'm not the only one. But it would be nice, wouldn't it, if everyone felt okay enough to stop hiding and come out from behind their brown chairs?

◆◆◆

Josephine
Teens

About the scene: Josephine remembers her driver's test. She was very nervous going into the test and tells an epic tale of how her driving inspector turned into a werewolf during her test.

Josephine:

Well, I remember something. My driver's test. And I always will, too. Because… because of what happened. And nobody here's going to believe me. But, well, I'll tell you anyhow. *(Takes breath.)* It started out okay. I mean, I was nervous about taking my driver's test, sure, but who isn't, right? So Mom drives me down to the place where they give the test, and she goes off to read a book or something. I'm standing there next to the car, and this guy comes out and he's carrying a clipboard with a pencil attached, and he says for me to get in the car.

Not "Howdy" or "Nice day" or anything. Just "Get in the car." So I do, and then he gets in. Then he asks me my name and stuff, and he's writing, and I sneak a little look at him. *(Shrugs.)* And he looks okay—I mean, for a skinny sour-puss. Then he says for me to start the car, so I start the car.

Then I'm supposed to drive straight ahead, so I look in the rear-view mirror, and I look all around, like I'm supposed to do, and I flip on my turn signal, you know, to tell everybody I'm coming out in that lane—only, I don't know, I flipped on the windshield wipers instead, and they're going like crazy and spraying water all over and wiping it off, and I finally find the switch and turn them off. "Just making sure the windshield's clean before we begin," I say pleasantly. And I give him a big grin, and he gives me this real icy stare out of his thick old glasses. But then I looked back at him because… because of his eyebrows. I hadn't noticed before, but, I don't know, now they seemed really big... and shaggy! Real shaggy!

Then he says, "Well, are we going?" And I say, "Yes sir. Right away, eyebrows. I mean—" We hadn't even left the curb, and I was in trouble. Anyway, I flipped on the right signal this time, which was really the left one, but, well, you get the idea, and I pulled out into traffic.

Well, I make it to the corner, I flip my signal, and I'm turning okay, but suddenly, I don't know, I go up over the curb! And it was a pretty high curb. Like maybe the Great Wall of China! Now, trust me, I've never gone over a curb before. Never! And I look over to tell him that, and he's writing like mad, of course. But now his clipboard looks about ten times bigger, and it's practically taking up the whole front seat, and his pencil is humongous, and he says for me to go to the stop sign then continue on.

So I do. But I'm going real slow now because I'm coming up to a stop sign, right? And some guy comes roaring up behind me, blasting his horn, and he yells at me to get out of his way and to turn off my signal, which I forgot and left on, and he's swearing at me, and it's just great. Road rage. I'm a victim of road rage and I haven't even gone a block! So now the guy next to me lets out this big groan and mutters something.

So I think, hey, maybe he's lightening up a little. And I smile and look to see if he's smiling too. He isn't. But then... then I notice the guy has these really strange teeth—like—like fangs, hanging out of his mouth. I'm not kidding—fangs! I hadn't noticed those before. And... and suddenly he's not quite talking the same either. I mean, now he sort of growls.

Well, with those fangs and those shaggy eyebrows and all, I'm too scared to look over his way before I turn. So now he really growls at me about not looking both ways before I turn. And I see he's writing like crazy on his great big clipboard, only— only now instead of hands—*(Shudders.)* he has big furry *(Gulps.)* paws! Paws, with sharp claws! Okay, okay, I know. But I saw them. And then I'm rolling through a stop sign, and he's growling at me for not making a complete stop.

And I know I did it wrong. But I just wanted to hurry and get this thing over with! And then he says something, only I don't hear him, and I forget and glance over his way and start to say, "Excuse me?" Only suddenly I can't say anything. I mean, I can't make a sound, because now the guy... *(Shudders and takes a breath.)* Now the guy has fur all over his forehead! And I'm going "Whoa!" What's going on here?!" And I'm trying to figure it out. And somehow I must have kept on driving and doing what he said, but I don't remember. Then, just to make sure, I peeked over at him again. And it was true. Just as I said. Shaggy eyebrows, big old fangs, furry paws, and furry forehead. *(Shudders.)* Oooh! And then, like a bolt of lightning, it hit me. This guy was turning into a werewolf! Right there in my mom's car! A werewolf! I had to get out of there... fast! Then I hear him sort of groaning that I should parallel park.

Parallel park? Parallel park with a werewolf in the car?! But I knew I had to do it because I wanted to get out of there. So I threw it into reverse, and then I threw it forward and then back again. Forward and backward, in and out, and I'm going really fast, and cars are going by me honking and yelling at me, and all the time the werewolf is making these sort of grunting sounds, like he's praying, or something, except he's a werewolf so he isn't.

And finally I head in and bang the curb with the front of the car, and the rear is still sticking out in traffic. But I don't care. It's the best I can do with a werewolf in the car. I turn off the motor, and I'm figuring out how I can escape fast, when right away, he opens the door and leaps out, growling something about how I failed—really failed, and then he just—vanishes, which is what werewolves do, I guess. *(Sighs.)* Anyway, when my mom comes to drive us home, I told her I failed. And I told her why. I tried to explain to her that this guy was a werewolf. Really! She said he didn't look like a werewolf to her. But she wasn't in the car. She doesn't know what really happened. But I know what happened. I was there. And I remember it. Well, I mean, let's face it. If a werewolf gave you a driver's test, wouldn't you remember it? Sure you would.

Melissa Anne
Teens

About the scene: Melissa Anne tells the group about her memories of her Uncle Jack. Everybody thought the world of Uncle Jack, but Melissa Anne hated him. Nobody in the family knew her secret—that when she was eight, he had tried to sexually abuse her.

Melissa Anne:

(With slight Southern accent.) I had an uncle, too. Uncle Jack. He'd come visitin' us once in a while. Everybody really liked my Uncle Jack. "Salt of the Earth," folks in town would say. He was my mama's older brother. We lived in this little town then, and Mama was really proud of Uncle Jack. He'd left right after high school and made it big up north somewhere. When Uncle Jack visited, he always brought lots of presents for us kids, and

other people, too. And well, like I said, everybody just thought the world of Uncle Jack. Except me. I hated him.

I was eight. I remember exactly because Uncle Jack had come down on one of his visits right near my birthday. After everybody had carried on about how good it was to see him, and after he'd given everybody their presents, Mama and Daddy went down to the store to get some ice cream so we could "celebrate proper," Mama said. And Austin and Joey—those were my little brothers— they went too so they could choose their own kind of ice cream on account of they were particular about that. Anyway, Mama said for me to stay home and keep Uncle Jack company.

After they left, Uncle Jack picked up the Barbie doll he'd brought me and started grinnin' and sayin' what a great build Barbie had and carrying on about this stupid doll. Then he puts me on his lap and says let's change her clothes. So I start takin' off the doll's clothes and he starts fiddlin' with mine. It was a real hot day—the way it gets in Mississippi in the summer— and I had on this little two-piece bathing suit. He was jokin' around askin' me what the top piece was for and stuff. He was laughin', and I remember I didn't think it was all that funny. But I laughed too, on account of he was Uncle Jack, and everybody in our house just automatically laughed at Uncle Jack's jokes. Then he says now that the doll's clothes are off, let's take mine off, too. Well, I got scared and tried to get down off his lap, only he was holding me real tight. And then he started pullin' my pants off, and I was really scared. I hit him and yelled for him to leave me alone! And then I got away, and I ran and hid in a closet. He found me and told me to come out, only I wouldn't.

Just then I heard our car comin' down the street, and I reckon he heard it, too. And I remember this like it was yesterday. He said, "Melissa Anne, don't you ever tell how we played, hear? 'Cuz you've been a naughty girl. And if you ever tell anybody, I'll tell on you. And then somethin' bad will happen." So I never told anybody. I knew nobody'd ever believe me anyhow, so what was the use of tellin'? And maybe somethin' bad would happen, like he said.

Well, Mama and Daddy came in with the ice cream, and Uncle Jack said he'd had a phone call from up north while they were gone. That was a lie. He said he had to leave right then and get back to his office. Mama was real upset, of course. Then she told me to kiss Uncle Jack goodbye and thank him for the nice doll he'd brought me. She didn't know I'd already thrown it away. He leaned down, but I turned my face away fast. Mama said I wasn't bein' very polite, and she apologized to Uncle Jack. He just smiled like nothin' had ever happened and said he'd see us again soon. As he was walking out onto the front porch, he chucked me under the chin and said in this low voice, "Don't forget what I said, honey." Then he got in his car and tooted his horn, like always, and waved, and Mama and Daddy and Austin and Joey were all standin' on the front porch, waving and hollerin' for him to come back soon, and Mama was blowin' kisses and everything. But I stayed inside, watchin' the ice cream melt. When Mama came back inside she said she didn't know what had gotten into me, I was actin' so ornery.

Well, about six months later Uncle Jack died in a car accident. They held the funeral in our town and everybody in the whole place, practically, turned out for it. Except me. I wouldn't go. Even made myself throw up all over my best dress so I wouldn't have to. Mama was just furious with me! "Nothin' is more important than family!" she hollered at me. "And you'll regret not goin' to your Uncle Jack's funeral someday, Melissa Anne. Yes, you will!" *(Sighs.)* Well, I don't regret it, and I never will. And I know Mama will never understand why.

Salem's Daughter

By Craig Sodaro

About the play: This suspenseful ghost story opens in 1692 when Sarah Brooks, who has been tried as a witch and sentenced to hang, curses those who would disturb her rest. Now jump to the present: every fall, popular Heather and her group of friends celebrate all of their birthdays at one communal party at Heather's house, which is built on the hill where the condemned witches were buried centuries earlier. Feeling the power of all being seniors in high school, Heather thought it would be a great prank to invite the new girl in town, an outcast named Sarah, to their birthday soiree. Heather insists that Sarah drink a glass of "Initiation Punch," but when Sarah collapses and dies, the joke suddenly stops. To protect their post-graduation dreams, the others decide to throw Sarah's body down the backyard well and vow never to tell anyone what happened. Jump forward another eight years: construction near the well has revealed… nothing. Even more unsettling, a police detective has told Heather that a woman in a long dress has been seen on her property. Is it Sarah? Or Sarah Brooks?

Time period: 1692 and the present.

Sarah Brooks
Early 20s - 40s

About the scene: At the beginning of the play, we're in the Meeting House in Salem in 1692, where Sarah Brooks is on trial for being a witch. She has just been condemned to death by Judge Markham, who marked her silence at the hearings as the "silence of evil when confronted with good." She will hang at dawn for her transgressions. In this monologue, Sarah addresses the judge and threatens to avenge whoever disturbs her rest.

Sarah Brooks:

Oh, this is a grand moment for you, Justice Markham. Another witch dispatched to punishment. One less troublesome soul wandering about the village. But where is your triumph, your honor? I am nothing but a poor woman whose husband died. I have no family left to rely on, so I have been forced to sell herbs and potions to those brave enough to buy my elixirs. It was all I could do to keep from starving. I live in the woods because that is where my poor husband built our house. He intended to clear a plot for farming, but fell ill before he could do so. I seldom come to the village because I do not have the appropriate dress. I know I am talked about. I have felt the laughter on my back as I walked the streets. True, I have no friends because no one in the village has courage. But I am no witch. Nor have I ever wronged anyone, in thought or word. I know you don't believe that because you have witnesses. You have those who judge only with their eyes, for they have no hearts. And they will go on living. As for me... you send me to my rest. I know it will be sweet, for I am tired. Too tired of breathing air contaminated by mistrust and deceit. I shall lie still and calm, and woe to he who touches my bones. Disturb me and my death will know no bounds! You hear that, Justice Markham? My death will know no bounds! *(Chuckles to herself.)*

Heather
18 years old

About the scene: Sarah feels awkward and imposing at the birthday party, knowing she doesn't belong there. However, Heather insists that Sarah blow out the candles on the cake and that they should all share what they wished for. Heather primes them to share their secrets by telling about her uncle, who wondered "if it was wrong to wish for something bad to happen to somebody."

Heather:

Remember my Uncle Bud?

When I was about ten or so, we went to a birthday party for Uncle Bud. There were all these sleazy people there. Mom hated to go to his parties, but Uncle Bud was her little brother and all that. Anyway, Uncle Bud was really nervous the whole time. Always kept looking out the windows. You know, like somebody was out there or something. Anyway, these four guys dressed in black brought out this big, fancy cake. I mean, this was a twelve-layer cake with enough frosting to cover Mt. Everest. Roses, angels, you name it swirled all over the top. Thirty candles blazed away on top. My grandmother told Uncle Bud to make a wish. He calmed down for just a minute and smiled. Then he blew out every candle. Later, I was playing Barbies in my cousin's room, and Uncle Bud was suddenly right there next to me. He had a habit of sneaking up, you know. Anyway, he sat on the bed and asked me if it was wrong to wish for something bad to happen to somebody at a birthday party.

I don't remember what I told him. I mean, Ken was about to ask Barbie out to the beach. I didn't care about Uncle Bud's problem, so I guess I must have said, "No." Anyway, then he acted real relieved, like I was his therapist or something. And he said he was sure God wouldn't make him suffer.

But three days later, Uncle Bud came over with presents for everybody. He was happier than I'd ever seen him in my whole life. I remember he brought me a new stereo. Can you believe it? My mom asked him what was up, and he said, "It isn't every day that Jimmy the Turk dies." I looked in the papers and sure enough, a big time hood named Jimmy the Turk had mysteriously fallen from the balcony of his penthouse, forty floors up.

My point is Uncle Bud wished for Jimmy the Turk to get killed— he told me his wish—and three days later it came true! [...]

Think about it. [...]

Well, we're all at least a little bit superstitious anyway, aren't we? Aren't you superstitious, Sarah?

The Secret Garden

Adapted by Gary Peterson

About the play: Mary, a lonely and spoiled orphan girl, arrives at Misselthwaite Manor to no fanfare. Her uncle is almost always away, made bitter by the loss of his wife during childbirth ten years earlier. Left to her own devices to entertain herself, Mary discovers a secret garden, once her deceased aunt's favorite place, but now shut off from the world. Mary also discovers her cousin Colin, a sickly boy who's always kept isolated. Mary's attention and nurturing, both for the garden and for Colin, creates magical transformations. In a touching climax, the garden's magic inspires the sickly Colin to walk and his stooped father to stand tall and learn to love again.

Time period: 1911.

Martha
20s or older

About the scene: Martha, the housemaid, tends to Mary, who has arrived at Misselthwaite Manor. Mary has just informed Martha that she always has someone dress her and that she doesn't know how to "play." Martha finds Mary, a spoiled child who was brought up in India, quite peculiar and attempts to get her to play as a child should.

Martha:

You never play? You don't play, you never dressed yourself— whatever did you do in that India place? […]

Oh, miss, if you don't remind me of one of them porcelain dolls what gets all dressed up fancy and then sits on a shelf! You need to get out of doors and smell the wild world. It's a fair lovely spring coming, and the earth's all awaking. What I wouldn't give to have the free time to go out and enjoy it. *(Struck.)* Wait a minute. I has summat for ye. Oh, I know I saw it in this room.

(Begins to open drawers in the dresser.) I noticed it when I was cleaning onest and it struck me as so odd. Why, here it is. *(Pulls a jump rope out of a drawer and displays it.)* Here it is. You could take this outside. […]

Why, it's a jump rope! What it's doing in here, I have no idea. But you can play with it. *(Stretches it out to MARY, but she doesn't take it.)* […]

Now don' tell me you've never played with a jump rope. […]

Oh, dear goodness! *(With that, she takes the jump rope in hand and begins skipping. After a moment, she begins to chant.)*

Silver bells,
Cockle shells,
Eevie, ivy, over.

I like coffee.
I like tea.
I like the boys,
And the boys like me.

Mother went to market
And got bread cheap.
Baby's in the cradle
Fast asleep.

A tiger chased me
Up a sycamore tree,
And this is what it said to me—

I like coffee.
I like tea.
I'd like Mary
To jump with me.

(Still skipping.) That's when you jump in, too. You say who you'd like to jump with you, and they jump in along with you. […]

It's the simplest game in the world. *(Stops.)* Oh, well, you take the rope, Mary—try it out yourself. Go outside and try it. You'll have fun.

Shakespeare by Monkeys
By Kamron Klitgaard

About the play: Some theories are nearly impossible to test, such as the Infinite Monkey Theorem, which states that a monkey, randomly hitting keys on a typewriter for an infinite amount of time, will eventually produce the complete works of William Shakespeare. Well, infinity isn't standing in the way of Dr. Hubble, who's determined to prove the theory correct by assembling a cast of zany assistants and six monkeys, whose only job is to get writing using a variety of writing devices!

Time period: The present.

Riley
20s - 30s

About the scene: Lab assistant Riley explains what motivated her to sign up for the project.

Riley:

No! I don't care about the money. I have a more noble purpose—I hate William Shakespeare!

In high school, they made us memorize Shakespeare passages and then recite them in front of the class. I'll never forget it… "This trusty servant shall pass between us. Ere long you are like to hear—if you dare venture in your own behalf—a mistress's command. Wear this. Spare speech. Decline your head. This kiss, if it durst speak, would stretch thy spirits up into the air."

And when I asked my teacher what it meant, she read the passage over several times, and then finally looked up at me and said, "I don't know." I don't know! Can you believe that? She's making me memorize it, and she doesn't even know what it means! It turns out that none of my college professors knew what it meant, either! I searched for the answer online. I searched for it in books. I took Shakespeare classes. No one in the world knows what it means!

But he's considered to be one of the greatest writers ever to live. He's forced on us in elementary school, middle school, high school, college! His plays are performed year after year the world over. Yet, he writes this incomprehensible dribble!

I figured if a monkey could write the complete works of William Shakespeare, then anybody could, proving he's no big deal.

Sir Huey and the Dragon

By Ryan Neely

About the play: Widowed King Arbitrary wants to find a husband for Princess Arabella and decides to do so in the most clueless way possible—pitting two knights against each other in feats of unimaginable danger and unlikely strength. But the wishy-washy king favors flashy Sir Truly over humble Sir Huey and stacks the deck against the nobler knight, sending him on a wild goose chase. Sir Huey still stands a fighting chance thanks to some help from a mysterious helmeted hero and some primitive tree gnomes. But it's Princess Arabella, who's in love with Sir Huey, who helps him in his quest for the heart of the fiery dragon.

Time period: Once upon a time...

Dragon
Ageless

About the scene: After eating the evil Sir Truly, Dragon calls on the village to change their ways and for King Arbitrary to allow his daughter to marry the righteous Sir Huey.

Dragon:

(Commandingly.) Everyone stop!

I'd like to say something. I believe... I believe you should all take a close look at yourselves and what you are doing. Is this really solving anything?

(Burps loudly.) Listen, if you'll just overlook the fact that I ate that cheating, lying knight, there is something to be said about non-violent resolutions. You, King Arbitrary, began all of this so that you could find someone worthy of your daughter's hand. Your daughter is already far braver than any of your knights because she fights for change. Well, I say, if being worthy of her

hand means to stand by her side, who is more worthy than the one man who shares her ideals? Who fights for truth and honor? Who cares not to kill wrongly? You can see that they have already chosen to stand by one another. Perhaps if you grant them the freedom to stay together, then together they can slay the true monster of this kingdom's narrow-minded intolerance and lack of unity. For you can't have strength in numbers if you don't allow those numbers to add up to anything. That's all...

(Burps.) Does anyone have an antacid?

The Snow White Variety Show

By Brian D. Taylor

About the play: On a TV talk show, the seven dwarves tell the story of Snow White as the Fairytale Players bring it to life. As each new dwarf takes a turn telling part of Snow White's famous story in his or her own unique voice, the players' re enactment shifts to match the style and personality of that particular dwarf. At any given moment, the story can be anything—romance, comedy, suspense, Western, home improvement show, epic poetry, mystery, cooking show, stand-up routine, or blockbuster action movie.

Time period: Once upon a time...

Evil Queen
40s - 50s

About the scene: In the style of a cooking show, the Evil Queen creates the poisoned apple.

Evil Queen:

Good evening, my pretties! And welcome to Wicked Stepmother's Kitchen! Today, we'll be stirring up the handiest little gem for knocking off your archenemy. It's an entrée I like to call The Apple of My... DIE! Mwa-ha-ha-ha! Now, for today's recipe, we start with your everyday, run-of-the-mill apple, and when we're done with it, it will be the most deadly apple you've ever known. […]

Now, this is truly the simplest recipe of them all! All it takes is a little inspiration, ingenuity, and the tiniest dash of revenge, and you have for yourself the deadliest fruit you'd ever imagine! *(Smiles.)* Now, as I said, you must start with your everyday, run-of-the-mill apple. But! There's a tiny skosh of prep work that needs to be done beforehand. And here's the secret to the magic. You see, the apple we'll be using for this recipe must be completely dehydrated beforehand. After all, if we want our little apple to be able to soak up every last ounce of liquid-death, we first need it to be completely void of all moisture. For this step, please help me welcome our special guest, the Big Bad Wolf!

(Big Bad Wolf enters.) Welcome, Wolfy! *(To audience.)* Now, as I was saying, we need this apple to be completely dehydrated. Wolfy, do your thing! *(Big Bad Wolf huffs and puffs and blows on the apple. Evil Queen reacts.)* And just like that we have the least juiciest apple you ever did see! Thank you, Wolfy! *(Big Bad Wolf bows and exits.)* Now, all it takes is a tiny bit of poison! Bottoms up! *(Smiles and pours the entire jug into the cauldron.)* A dash of salt... mix gently... *(Puts the oar in and mixes the concoction methodically.)* And now we wait for six short hours while our thirsty little apple does its magic. *(Waits and looks at her watch. After just the right amount of awkward time...)* And, voila! *(Pulls out the apple and holds it up.)* A poisoned apple that's certain to knock 'em dead at your next gathering! Care for a taste?

Join us next time, when we uncover the lost art of freshly baked gingerbread and the enticing effects it has on innocent little children who are lost in the woods! Until next time, I'm Evil Stepmother saying, "Good food means good riddance!" Goodbye until next time on Wicked Stepmother's Kitchen!

◆◆◆

Staying Home

By Ev Miller

About the play: This play concerns the impact of an unplanned baby on the lives of two teens. It's vacation time, so Lisa is looking forward to seeing her best friends. After all, so much has happened over the past few months. Everyone has ventured off to college... except for Lisa. An unplanned pregnancy forced her and Mark to make different choices. Although the two are now married, the birth of Megan has forced them to change their aspirations. Lisa no longer fits in with her friends and their new lives. When she realizes that she cannot turn back the pages of time, she is better able to appreciate the special things in her life with less regret.

Time period: The present.

◆◆◆

Lisa
18 - 19

About the scene: Lisa's friends have left and she shares her thoughts aloud with her baby.

Lisa:

Hi, sweetheart. Sleeping so hard. Oh, Megan, what happened to my life? I love you so much, but I wanted to go to college, too. Did you know that your mommy was the best student in high school? *(Picks the baby up, cooing softly.)* That's right... I was. My mommy and daddy wanted me to go to an Ivy League school. They always had such big plans for me. They wanted me to be a lawyer, just like my daddy... your grandpa is. But then you came along. *(Softly crying.)* Oh, it isn't your fault. I just fell crazy in love with your daddy and one thing led to another. Someday, when you fall in love, you'll understand. My mommy and daddy sure don't. I guess they've forgotten what it's like to be young and in love. But I'm going to be a good mommy to you, Megan, and a good wife to your daddy. Maybe someday I'll have the chance to go to college, too, but it will just have to wait, won't it?

Stopping at Ellis Island

By Thomas Hischak

About the play: In a room on Ellis Island in 1906, seven newly-arrived immigrants have been singled out by the authorities and told to wait. These detainees from Italy, Ireland, Norway, and Russia are fearful of being rejected and sent back to Europe. As they wait, the immigrants begin to build a kinship with each other. The lucky immigrants who are declared healthy exit to be processed, bringing to life the hopes and dreams of the millions of Europeans who immigrated to America at the turn of the century.

Time period: 1906.

Katie
20s

About the scene: Katie is an immigrant from Ireland. Here, she sits in a waiting room on Ellis Island with other hopeful immigrants, all waiting to enter America. Katie sends her "good-riddance" to Ireland, a land where there's nothing but rain and false pots of gold, as she addresses another immigrant.

Katie:

(With an Irish accent.) Well, I don't mind telling you that where I come from in Ireland it was only fit for a pig to live. Not that we could afford any pigs. It was all mud and rain, but nothing grows. And the wind is fierce in the winter and it burns your face in summer, and the storms from the sea were enough to— […]

So here I am. You won't catch me crying for the old sod. All that about the Emerald Isle sitting like a jewel in the sea? Pure blarney. And the leprechauns with their crocks of gold, sitting there at the end of a rainbow? […]

The rainbow is a fake caused by all the mist, and the gold is lead like the crock is lead. I'll tell you what's so grand about Ireland. It's a grand place to leave!

Stuck

By Jon Jory

About the play: This play takes place in the COVID era, during a stay-at-home order. Each character is school-aged and shares their feelings of being stuck at home. Some are bored and eager for any human interaction outside their family, while others are quite productive in what they're doing with their time while cooped up at home.

Time period: 2020.

Melissa
13 - 16

About the scene: Melissa explains to the audience how being quarantined changed how she understands her family.

Melissa:

Well, what I would say is there's nothing like staying at home for three months to help you figure out your family. When I look back, I'd have to say I just didn't take them seriously. My family, I mean. I think maybe I thought they were just like the furniture that you had to look out you didn't bump into.

I mainly took my dad to be like a firework you had to be careful not to light up. My mom was just what made it all go, but I don't think I saw her beyond that. My sister, Ellie, was poison ivy, and my older brother, Comet, was a ride to school and a loud noise around the house.

I guess you could say I was so self-concerned, I didn't know who anybody was. Well, surprise, surprise! They're human beings! I mean, I started really watching them like I was on a visit to the zoo, and it turns out they're complicated. Who would have guessed? How I started to see them was this rule I made up for myself called "The Six Things." It just hit me. I was mainly seeing them as one thing, which boiled them right down to nearly invisible.

So I said to myself, "Melissa," which is my name for myself, though I'm Suzy on my birth certificate, "Melissa, what six things is Ellie today?" Like yesterday she was scared, bossy, funny, smart, fed up, and clumsy. Shoot, I could have put down ten things if that was in my rules. The day before, she was five entirely different things, but still bossy.

Now, you're going to think I'm out of my mind, but I don't think I knew my family was complicated. What I found out, which has kind of changed my life, is that they are interesting! They're surprising! I mean, some days, they are actually worth being around.

I forget that woman's name who went to some country or other and spent most of her life living with apes. You know who I mean. Well, it turns out my family is just as interesting as apes! Seriously. They are. So I wake up every morning, bounce out of bed and say to myself, "Melissa, let's get downstairs and see what the gorillas are up to!" I hate to say this, but I'm enjoying it.

Unnamed
Teens

About the scene: The speaker remembers the loss of her sister.

Unnamed:

About two weeks after they said people had to stay home, we found out my sister wasn't going to make it. She had something they call Reye's syndrome that causes swelling in the liver and brain. She was no holds barred stubborn about wanting to stay home. She said dying was strange enough without doing it in a strange place with strangers.

My mom is an ICU nurse so home is where she stayed. Her room had pink and white striped wallpaper and a ceiling with stars on it that glowed in the dark. She had every album Taylor Swift ever made, and they played all day. She said Taylor Swift was going to sing her out.

We have two dachshunds named Lucy in the Sky and Imagine, and those dogs would get up on that bed with her and snuggle right close until she went to sleep at night. She told me not to be sad because she'd had a really good time every day of her life not counting the last two weeks. She didn't feel like talking too much, but she wanted us to. She said she was holding on to our voices. She said the words were keeping her with us as long as possible before she left on her journey.

So Mom and Dad and me and Grandma, who was staying with us, just kept the words going and didn't let the silence in. Mom stayed in there with her all night sitting in a rocking chair Grandpa had made. She had us all write messages to her on her sheets that she could take with her on her travels. We each wrote one every day.

I remember on her last Wednesday, I asked her how she was doing, and she said she had finished packing her bags. She said she was sorry for the trouble, but I had to live two lives now because she was leaving me hers. When she was gone, the two dachshunds howled. So did I, but I did it inside where you couldn't hear it. There is more to silence than you think.

Tested

By Kendra Thomas

About the play: Standardized testing is all about rules and protocol. Two #2 pencils. Sanctioned calculators. Carefully filled-out Scantrons. But is standardized testing really fair when the students themselves are anything but "standard"? Sure, for some it's no big deal—testing is just a chance to earn ice cream or cash rewards from their parents when they do well. But then there are those with dyslexia, test anxiety, ADHD—as the students hit the panic button, it takes their caring teacher to remind and reassure the class that each of them is far more than just a test score.

Time period: The present.

Abigail
Teens

About the scene: Abigail shares with the audience about her dyslexia and how it makes testing difficult for her, especially since her parents don't want her "labeled" as dyslexic.

Abigail:

So... I'm probably severely dyslexic. Probably. That's what they told my parents two years ago. They said I should get tested, get diagnosed, and then get the help I needed to do good in school. I mean, it's only a stupid label, right? The other kids with those labels get to go to a special class and get help. They get more time for their tests, and one of my friends doesn't even have to write down the answers. He says them to a teacher, and they write them down for him! But my parents? They didn't want me to have to live with the... *(Does air quotes.)* ...stigma. I'm not even sure what that means. Sounds like a sting. A little bite you put some cream on and it eventually heals. Stigma. I get it. They want to protect me. And sometimes, I'm okay with that. But on test days like this?

The teachers can't even help me understand the directions because technically I'm a regular kid without any problems. I'm supposed to just get it and not need any help. But I'm so lost! Sometimes I just bubble in the answers to get it over with. I know I won't pass. I hope it doesn't matter that I don't pass. I really don't want it to matter.

I don't think I'd mind being diagnosed dyslexic. I wrestle with writing and reading every day—it's like a dragon I have to face. And don't you need a sword to slay a dragon? I feel like having a label would give me a sword... some help... a weapon to fight my struggles...

Anyway, facing these tests? That's like facing a beast. Like being expected to slay a dragon. *(Holds up her fists.)* I guess I have to do the best I can without the armor and sword.

Thistle Blossoms

By Roseanna Beth Whitlow

About the play: The show examines the relationship that develops between a troubled student and a rigid university instructor. Their conflict begins as Lisa walks into Jo's classroom on the first day of spring break. It is their first encounter since Lisa turned in her personal essay assignment—a work describing her own planned suicide, aborted only by Jo's intervention.

Time period: The present.

Lisa
18 - 22

About the scene: Lisa reads Jo her journal entry describing how she would commit suicide.

Lisa:

"On weekends, while everyone else is partying or shopping or dating, I go to Eagle Park, the one where they have all the beer busts and fraternity parties. Only I go after the parties are over and everyone has gone. The grass is littered with cans and bottles and crumpled up plastic cups and an occasional T-shirt or tennis shoe that someone left behind. The trees' lower branches are broken and look sad and lonely. I feel at home there, among the cast-offs and trash. I fit in with the ugly thistles that grow along the creek… them and their ridiculous blossoms.

"It was there on a Saturday morning, amidst the leavings of an all-night party, that I decided to do it. I felt an instant relief. But it would take planning. I had to decide how to do it. There are so many ways, and they've all been tried by people just like me. I decided against all the cop-out methods—the suicides people accuse you of trying when you don't really want to die. Ways like pills or exhaust fumes or even hanging. A gun is for real. No backing out. No changing your mind. You pull that trigger, and you're gone. So when I went home last time, I found my dad's gun. He wouldn't miss it. He never uses it. It does feel strange to touch a gun. It's cold and much heavier than you'd think from watching TV shows or movies. But I got used to it. It became my friend. With it, I could share my secret plan. On the first day of spring break, we—my gun and me— *(With a catch in her throat, Jo corrects her grammar.)* —my gun and I will go to Eagle Park, and I will really become part of the lonely litter, lying in the grass like a crumpled, discarded cup."

And then there was a note to you about how I liked your class and thanking you for taking an interest in my writing.

Jo
30s - 60s

About the scene: Jo confronts Lisa after Lisa claims that her suicide would not affect anyone.

Jo:

How dare you joke about it? How dare you think about doing that to me? Or to them? Haven't you been listening at all? […]

You paint such a romantic picture of Lisa's suicide. And it ends like an old technicolor movie. Poor Lisa, found lying in the wildflowers at the park, lying crumpled up like a discarded Dixie cup. Well, reality isn't that romantic. It isn't that pretty. In fact, what you leave behind for us isn't pretty at all. Do you know what it's really like to have someone you know and care about commit suicide? When he stacks his books around him, sticks a gun in his mouth, and blows the back of his head away?

First, there's the denial. You hear rumors, but it can't be him. Then the truth comes, but you still say, "No, that can't be. I just saw him yesterday." Then the reality, all of the cruelty of the world hits. The cold, impersonal funeral—suicides are an embarrassment to everyone, you know. You hear people who don't even know him make crude, off-handed remarks about the mess he must have made, with the blood and the matter. And always there's the self-blame. "Why wasn't I there?" you say. "I could have stopped this." You torment yourself with the tiniest of details—the time you were in too much of a hurry to talk, a thoughtless remark you may have made. But mostly you relive his death over and over in your mind. You can't stand the sound of firecrackers, and the slamming of a door makes you jump, and your mind jumps back to what you imagine must have been the last second that he lived and breathed and thought and felt. It's that second before, and the anguish he must have felt. That exact second before he—pulled... that... trigger. The trigger that ended his life—and killed that part of me that lived in him. Yes, that part of my life that involved him is all gone. And I'll spend the rest of my life with a part of me that will never live or feel or laugh again. So, you see, when you kill yourself, you kill a little part of everyone you know.

◆◆◆

The Turret Rose

By David F. Strandin

About the play: Catherine is a twelve-year-old crippled girl who spends her days in a small turret atop her family's old home. There the light shines on her face again. In this make-believe world, Catherine pulls out costumes from her grandmother's trunk and imagines herself a princess in a glittering dance hall, dancing with handsome gentlemen and brave princes. But downstairs her mother, father, and older sister, Lucille, face the news that Catherine's condition is worsening, and that she will die soon.

Time period: 1970s.

◆◆◆

Adeline
30s - 40s

About the scene: The girls' mother, Adeline, describes to Lucille the family's beautiful rose garden that was blooming when Catherine was born.

Adeline:

(Dreamily.) And the rose garden in the backyard. Such pretty roses. They just don't seem to grow here. Your father says the ground isn't right, too rocky or something. But weren't those the prettiest roses? I remember how proud I was of them the year Catherine was born, just the week before she was born, the bushes filled with the biggest buds. And the morning I went to the hospital… on the way… I remember seeing how gloriously the buds had begun to blossom. There was one, a big red one. So like velvet. Your father brought it to me in the hospital. The first thing I saw in my room after Catherine was born, the first thing I saw was that rose, that beautiful rose. I was so happy… and then your father came in with the doctor. *(Puts her fist to*

her mouth.) And they told me about Catherine. (*Stifles a sob.*) Strange how quickly that rose withered. By the next day, its petals had almost all fallen onto the tabletop. (*Sighs, lowering arm.*) Oh, yes, Lucy dear, I remember. (*Softly.*) I remember.

◆◆◆

Catherine
12 years old

About the scene: Catherine talks to a pretend friend, Elsie, that she has created in her mind from a paper princess. During this monologue, one idea seems to evolve freely from another.

Catherine:

Don't you just love when it's evening, Elsie? And everything turns red, like everything is part of a big, beautiful flower, blossoming, getting bigger and bigger until even the trees, especially the fall colored trees, are a part of it.

You do? I'm glad.

You like it as much as you like your name? (*Laughs.*) You are a funny lady… and a fine lady.

And a dancing lady, too? Oh, yes.

And you like him, too. Oh, yes, he's very nice. He even kissed my hand once… just like in a fairy tale. And I was a princess.

Like you are.

Yes, your highness, I'll come and sit by you and sing a dancing song. (*With great effort, she steps down the rungs of the ladder, almost stumbling once, but catching herself, obviously in great pain. She sits before the paper princess named Elsie, trying first to curtsy, but stumbling again.*) Yes, your highness, I'll sing you a dancing song until he comes. He did say he was coming back, didn't he?

Oh, yes, before night. I like nighttime, don't you? *(Touches the paper arm of the figure.)* I knew you liked nighttime, Princess Elsie. *(Hugs herself.)* Because nighttime's a wishing time, and wishes do come true.

Star bright, star of night, I wish I may, I wish I might, have the wish I wish tonight.

And wishes do come true.

Yes, I'll sing a dancing song... until he comes.

The Virtual Family

By Jeremy Johnson

About the play: Meet the Virtuals—Dad, Mom, Son, Daughter, Grandma, plus a cat named Kitten and a kitten named Cat. Part Griswalds, part Jetsons, they're just an ordinary family living in extraordinary times during a world pandemic. A slew of technological advances, electronic home assistants, and computerized appliances, including Bobert the vacuum and FAB, the Fitness Assistant Bot, are meant to make life easier and bring the Virtuals together, but somehow they wind up more disconnected than before! Maybe technological advances aren't all they're cracked up to be?

Time period: 2020.

Daughter
Teens

About the scene: During the pandemic, Daughter frets in her diary over the difficulties of online school.

Daughter:

Dear Diary, more than month into this whole homeschooling experiment and I seriously think I'm losing it. I'm doomed to spend the rest of [insert grade level here] at home. The cats spend all day chasing each other and getting into fights. And then Mom has her tone with people on the phone—you know, that kind of sarcastic way of talking that the family knows really well but that the person on the other end probably thinks is really pleasant. Believe me, it's not. Good thing you can't see her expression! And last but not least there's Dad, typing so obnoxiously on his computer. Ugh. We get it, Dad, you can type sixty words a minute! Big whoop! Do you really have to do it so loudly? I'm trying to do work, people! And if that isn't bad enough, Dad cut our internet off today with his stupid hedge trimmers and so I had to do my math assignment on actual paper, and then take a picture of it with my phone and email it to my teacher like some Neanderthal. It was so embarrassing!

In fairness to Mom and Dad, it's not like there aren't a million more distractions. I do like to take too many breaks to play with Freddie. He's only a kitten, but he's already so big! He's like the little brother I never had. And I just love to scoop him up and pet his ridiculously furry tail! Sometimes the cats stare out the window at the family of finches that nest every year in our gutter. Did you know that finches in the U.S. were only pets until a bunch of pet stores in New York released them into the wild in the 1940s? Now they're everywhere! Anyhow, I like to watch the cats watch the finches. And sometimes I like to watch the finches too. Their song is so nice. It's not distracting at all. But then the squirrels get involved. And by mid-day the mailman comes and rattles the mailbox…

(Sighs.) I like learning. Especially reading and writing and specials. Ooh, and science! And Mom and Dad do a really good job helping. Really, they do. They're both so smart! Even though Dad likes to pretend he's kind of dumb. But it's just so hard to do it all on my own. I know the other kids in my class are probably feeling the same way. I just wish I had a chance to be with them again so we could talk about it. Like, "Why can't Miss Carrie figure out how to use Google Docs?" Or "Did you see how Coach T misspelled 'exersize'? Good thing he's a gym teacher, right?" I know we'll all see each other again soon, but I just… I just feel so alone right now. I've got my family, but I miss my friends.

◆◆◆

The Waiting Room

By Noah Bennett

About the play: In a simple waiting room, people arrive at their appointed time to face the unknown of what lies beyond an ominous closed door. Earl Trent, an older man, arrives early and is instructed by the businesslike receptionist to wait till his time. Scared about why he was summoned to the waiting room, he encounters people of all ages arriving at their assigned time. From all walks of life, each person he meets has followed a unique journey to get to this moment... their time to die. Some never saw it coming, others knew all too well that their time was coming, and a few even welcomed it. Through his encounters with the others in the waiting room, Earl gains both insight and courage about the meaning of life.

Time period: The present.

Granddaughter
20s - 30s

About the scene: Granddaughter is the caretaker for her blind grandmother, who also has many other health problems. Granddaughter is confused because she has received a telegram as well her grandmother. While Grandmother uses the restroom, Granddaughter talks to Earl, who is also waiting for his appointment time.

Granddaughter:

Death has been knocking on her door for a long time, if you know what I mean, but what I don't understand is, why did I get a telegram, too? It's not like I'm the one in need of this. My poor grandma struggles every day of her life, and I know, because I'm right by her side every single day. She is literally walking into death blind. A task as simple as putting her clothes on and getting her up and down the stairs every day can become such a big, life-threatening production. I have to clean the house constantly, because even the slightest bit of dust will send her emphysema haywire. You're familiar with emphysema, right? I mean it's that and her eyesight and just more and more health problems every day. I don't know how much more she can take. All of this, though, has taught me not to take life for granted.

But it can also be a curse. Life is just one giant game. No matter how hard you try to win, you can't. Do you know who wins? Death! Death always wins! Death is just one giant black hole, and it's just a matter of who gets sucked in next! Most of us believe that death is nothing but a curse, but some see it as a gift. I hate to say it, but in my grandmother's case, it'll be a gift. God, I really hope she's okay.

Walkin' Home

By Steven Orth

About the play: Sonja was a rebellious child who left home at the age of 17. Ever since then, her father has stared out the window, waiting for her to return. After a two-year downward spiral, she now stands on her old front porch, contemplating her decision to walk through the door again. Her travel companion, Stan, attempts to dissuade her from returning by reminding her why she left in the first place. Meanwhile, inside the house, her parents, George and Jenny, and her older sister, Nora, are preparing Thanksgiving dinner. Through flashbacks, the audience learns the struggles they all have had both before and after Sonja left. The story ends as Sonja walks through the door with the hope of a different, better relationship with her mother, father, and sister—one for which they, too, have been yearning.

Time period: The present.

◆◆◆

Nora
22 years old

About the scene: Nora, Sonja's older, responsible sister, resents tremendously the amount of attention her father still devotes to Sonja, even though Nora has been the one at home helping him. Here, she vents her frustrations to her mother.

Nora:

What I understand is that he loves a daughter who was never here when he needed her to help out at work. She was never here when he needed someone to help around the house or to make him dinner. Where was she when the business was in trouble and someone had to take over the finances? Where was she when he collapsed from exhaustion? Where was she when he got rushed to the emergency room? Who rode in the ambulance?

Held his hand and told him it would be all right? Me, that's who. I never said no to him. Anything he ever asked for, I did. Any time he ever needed, I gave. I have spent my life trying to be the "good daughter" but— *(Her anger is changing to bitterness.)* — look at him. All he can do is sit there as if the world no longer exists without her. Guess what, Mom? He has ignored you, too. Neither of us can compare to her.

Sonja
19 years old

About the scene: Sonja talks to her former self on the day she left home. She wishes she had listened to her parents and stayed. If only she had known then what she knows now—if only her latter self could have talked to the former to warn her in advance of the trials and tribulations ahead. Stan, who had first persuaded her to leave with him two years ago, listens nearby.

Sonja:

You think you're so smart, don't you? […]

You will never have it better than you do right now. All that money in that check in your right front pocket won't last 90 days. You'll blow a chunk of it on a brand new sportscar that you'll crash—without insurance, of course. Then you'll lose another chunk of it in legal fees from the little old lady who sues you for damages resulting from the accident. Without your license—which you'll lose, too—you'll have to buy bus tickets and pay for taxis to get to all of those amazing places you think you are headed. Oh, yes, don't forget all those new "friends" you'll make at the bars and parties—you'll buy them round after round, then wake up the next morning with your bags dumped everywhere and your cash missing. After that, you'll have to hitchhike to get anywhere. Yeah, that'll be fun, even exciting, for a while, until you realize how creepy the guys are that pull over to offer you a ride. Then, you'll start to walk to get to your destinations. Problem is, you won't be able to think of anywhere you actually want to go. The reality of your "new life" will have sunk in, and you'll wonder what you'll have to do to get by— how many days you can realistically survive without food until you give in and wander into a mission for some free soup. One night, as you sit outside in the pouring rain with nowhere else to sleep, you'll look up at an odd billboard with a photo of a man that looks strikingly familiar and has the word "home" plastered across the bottom. Only then will you remember the words he spoke to you just now and realize that— *(Glances at Stan.)* —despite the recommendations of others, the only place you should go is the one place you swore you'd never go back to again. […]

(To Stan.) If I didn't remember being her, I'd swear that I almost believe she could make it. All she—I—had to do was turn around, just then, and none of this would have happened. The last two years would have been different… better. […]

I wish I had never left and… I wish I had never met you. *(Stan is shocked by what he just heard.)* There, I said it. So will you just leave me alone now?

Jenny
40s

About the scene: Jenny, Nora and Sonja's mother, explains to her older daughter that it isn't about longing or wishing for Sonja's return, it's believing in it. With faith in unconditional love and support, she now shares their father's deep conviction that Sonja will come home when she is ready.

Jenny:

One thing has become abundantly clear to me—no amount of anger, tears, or regret will bring your sister home. I've pleaded with your father to forget her and move on with our lives. We still have you to make us proud. And you have, so many times over. Yet, he insists that she will return to us, some day. In this he possesses the deepest conviction. In all of our years together, I have never seen him express so stout a belief. Over time, he has worn down all of my anger, my fear, my worry. His steadfast resolve has become my own. I, too, believe that she'll be back. [...]

The other day, I was driving home from the mall when I got caught in the rush hour jam on the freeway. For 20 minutes, not even the squirrels in the trees moved. I looked out the passenger side window and saw a billboard of a young girl who reminded me of Sonja. With the trees covering part of the slogan, all I could read was the word "unconditional." Something inside of me just turned... around. I can't explain it. After two years' time, I just know that I am ready for her to come home.

War Letters

By J. Robert Wilkins

About the play: A man is off on a peacekeeping mission overseas. The women Jack leaves at home must deal with his six month absence, each facing the reality of separation privately. Their only connection with the man they love is via letters. Through this correspondence, the audience becomes privy to their fears, their hopes, their anticipation, and ultimately... their sorrow. His wife, Karen, must take charge of the household and the family for the first time in her married life. Lillian, his mother, is haunted by the memories of losing Jack's father in the Korean War. His daughter, Mary, struggles with her bitterness regarding her father's absence as well as the reason behind it. This drama powerfully depicts not only the sacrifices made by soldiers but also by their families.

Time period: 1990s.

◆◆◆

Karen
Mid 30s

About the scene: Karen writes a letter to her husband, Jack, uncertain whether to be honest about her feelings or remain upbeat for Jack's sake.

Karen:

(Writes a letter.) My dearest Jack. It is hard to believe that you have been gone six weeks already. I thought that it would get easier as the time went by, but that is not the case. It is difficult being both mother and father to Mary. *(Crumples the letter. She takes another piece of paper, sighs, and writes again.)* My dearest Jack. Another week has passed. In less than five months you will be home again. Mary and I are doing fine. We have finished digging up the garden and have all the vegetables stored in the cold room. Mary has been such a big help. She is growing up so

quickly. I am sure you will notice a difference in her when you return. We have put all the garden tools away including the lawn mower. I hope we put them all in the right places. I guess we will find out next spring when you go to bring them out. Our snow shovel looks pretty awful. I think Mary and I will go shopping for a new one this weekend. There is no snow in the forecast but you know how quickly the weather can change here. Mary is going to a school dance this Friday night. She has been busy all week deciding what to wear. And, of course, she has a hair appointment right after school on Friday. As you can imagine she seems to be on the phone constantly this past week. I will drive her and a couple of her friends to the school. Then I will pick them up afterwards. She is very excited.

(She stops.) Oh, Jack. Why do you have to miss all this?

Mary [1]
13 years old

About the scene: Mary addresses the audience, revealing her worry for her father being overseas fighting in the war. Mary had always felt comforted knowing her Dad was in the house when he was at home. Now, she isn't necessarily frightened that he's away, she is just uncomfortable without him at home.

Mary:

(Hugs her teddy bear.) I caught Mom crying last night. She was writing a letter to Dad. She tried to stop when I came in, but she couldn't help herself. We had a long talk about Daddy being overseas. When I asked her why she was crying, she said that some days being without Daddy gets her down. She seemed frightened, although she tried hard not to show it. She asked me how I felt. I told her that I missed Daddy very much, especially

in the evenings. I never realized how safe I felt just knowing that he was in the house. I don't really feel frightened now that he is not here. I guess I feel uncomfortable. Maybe that's how Mom feels. Maybe she's not frightened at all.

◆◆◆

Mary [2]
13 years old

About the scene: At Christmas time, Mary writes a letter to her father, who is stationed overseas.

Mary:

(Puts on a small locket. Writes a letter.) Dear Dad. Thank you so much for the Christmas presents. I like every single one. I especially liked the one you sent from over there. It was so special because I know you picked it out just for me. *(Fingers the locket.)* I am going to put yours and Mom's picture in it. That way you will always be with me. I really missed having you here at Christmas. I have done a lot of thinking about things over the holidays. I wonder if people really believe all this "Peace on Earth" stuff. I know that where you are, Christians are fighting each other. If they really believed that peace was that important, don't you think they would find another way to resolve their differences? And what really gets me is how everyone says they are fighting with God on their side. How can that be? I can't believe God wants anybody to kill babies. I hope you and all the other peacekeepers can put a stop to all of this nonsense. It would be nice if everyone practiced peace on Earth. Then you wouldn't have to be away from us... ever.

◆◆◆

Whispers

By Kendra Thomas

About the play: Alone in a small wood, Kate grieves the death of her dad—an Iraq war casualty—while lamenting a looming move to Texas with her newly widowed mother. A special place Kate once shared with her father, the familiar forest is now filled with the whispered memories of other "military brats" like her who have also lost parents in combat. The Whispers are the only ones who seems to fully fathom the pain of losing a parent when you're still a child. And it's only by sharing their stories that they can be sure to never forget.

Time period: 2018.

Kate
Teens

About the scene: Kate is reflecting as she stands in the middle of a grove of pecan trees, the special place where she and her father used to go together. The Whispers around her have told their stories of how they lost their own parents, and Kate realizes it's now her turn to share her own story.

Kate:

I've listened to all of your stories. I think there's a piece, a whisper of me in each one—a fragment of the way I feel. Jenny, I'll never forget the day my dad died, and I'm also afraid to forget the happy moments. Jason, there's not a day that goes by that I don't wonder, "What if?" Dane, it's those happy, funny moments I'll miss most, like catching fireflies by the lake together and my dad's arms wrapped around me in a bear hug so tight that I felt I was the safest kid in the world. Marie, I'd give anything to feel normal again. And Hayden, I like your drawing. I think your mom will like it, too. My mom and I made a teddy bear from one of my dad's old t-shirts, and I sleep with it every night. Maybe I can help you make one? Kelly, thank you for reading your letter. I don't know if I'm ready yet, but I'll try to write to my dad, too. There are some things I need to say, some things I need to tell him before I forget.

And my story? Well, we're moving. We're moving tomorrow, and it's all my dad's fault. I didn't tell anyone. Not even my best friend. I don't want her to lose me like I lost my dad. And sometimes I think it's easier to not talk about it, not talk about anything that hurts us. […]

But now I have to talk. I have to tell someone. I can't let people forget. And if we all remember, then I can heal. Then my dad died for something real—a memory. A memory of the cost of war. A memory of the price we pay for freedom.

My name is Kate Iverson. My dad died in Iraq while on patrol in a civilian neighborhood. He was shot four times—once through the heart. He was 35 years old. *(Looks at a photograph of her father.)* Dad, Mom and I are moving away. We're going to Texas to be near Grandma and Grandpa, but I promise that no matter where I go, I won't forget you. And I promise to share your memory no matter how much it hurts. I won't let us forget. None of us will ever forget. *(Kisses the photograph.)* I love you, Daddy. I miss you.

Why Darkness Seems So Light

By Helen Frost and Harvey Cocks

About the play: Here is a chilling look at the violence that pervades teenagers' lives, regardless of their social status or upbringing. Based on the writings of 250 high school students, the play is a stirring series of linked scenes depicting the effects of violence on young people, their families, and others around them. While the topic is heavy and intended for mature audiences, the play is not depressing. It introduces a sense of hope that the love of parents, siblings, friends, and teachers can help teens through experiences of violence and rough times.

Time period: The present.

Mrs. Appleton
40s - 50s

About the scene: Mrs. Appleton is a teacher at the local high school. One of her students, Johnny, was recently shot and killed during an altercation at a party, a victim of being in the wrong place at the wrong time. The police are looking for witnesses, but everyone who was involved is too afraid to step forward. Mrs. Appleton thinks aloud about her students. She regrets that even though she wants to help them, there's little she can do, and in her role as a teacher, she even makes things worse.

Mrs. Appleton:

(Cutting an article out of a newspaper.) I don't know why I save all these articles. I have a file folder full of them—things my students have been involved in. *(Holds up a file folder full of newspaper articles. Puts the new clipping in it.)* And these are just the ones I know about, the ones who have been caught. Johnny was in my class. He'd been coming to class once or twice a week. I'm sure Tank knows something about this, but

of course I can't ask him about it. Even Ginger seems unusually distracted this week.

Who can these kids talk to? I start the year with 30 students in each class, and I try to keep track of all of them, but it gets overwhelming. Usually I don't know why they stop coming to school. It just happens gradually. Something happens at home or on the streets, and they miss a day or two, and then they're behind when they come back. They miss four or five assignments and their grades slide. I hate to give out D's and F's, but if they don't do the work, I don't have any choice. And then they see the F, they start thinking they're a failure, what's the use, and it's a downward slide from there. It's heartbreaking.

Womanspeak

By Gloria Goldsmith

About the play: A Contemporary Woman is in search of her roots. Out of the past, Abigail Adams, Sojourner Truth, Susan B. Anthony, Margaret Sanger, Eleanor Roosevelt, and others show her that she is part of a great tradition of women who contributed to history.

Time period: 1850.

Sojourner Truth
53 years old

About the scene. Sojourner Truth speaks at a Women's Rights Convention.

Sojourner Truth:

Well, children, where there is so much racket, there must be something out of kilter. I think 'twixt the Negroes of the South and the women of the North, all talking about rights, the White men will be in a pretty fix soon. But what's all this here talking about? That man out there says that women need to be helped into carriages and lifted over ditches, and to have the best place ever'where. Nobody ever helps me into carriages, or over mud puddles, or gives me any best place! An' ain't I a woman? Look at me! Look at my arm! I have ploughed and planted, and gathered into barns, and no man could heed me! And ain't I a woman? I could work as much and eat as much as a man... when I could get it... and bear the lash as well! And ain't I a woman? I have borne thirteen children and seen them most all sold off to slavery, and when I cried out with my mother's grief none but Jesus heard me! And ain't I a woman? Then that little man out there, he says women can't have as much rights as men 'cause Christ wasn't a woman! Where did your Christ come from? From God and a woman! Man had nothing to do with Him. […]

If the first woman God ever made was strong enough to turn the world upside down all alone, these women together ought to be able to get it right side up again.

The Wonderful Wizard of Oz

Adapted by Tim Kelly

About the play: A cyclone carries Dorothy and her dog, Toto, to the magical land of Oz, where they encounter all the familiar characters from the beloved story... the Cowardly Lion, the Tin Woodsman, the rubber-legged Scarecrow, Glinda the Good Witch, and the Wicked Witch of the West, who is determined to destroy Dorothy and steal the silver slippers.

Time period: Once upon a time...

Wicked Witch
Ageless

About the scene: Dorothy and Scarecrow, Tin Woodsman, and the Cowardly Lion have just met with the great Oz. He commands them to search for the Wicked Witch and destroy her before he'll grant them their wishes. Here, the Wicked Witch watches the group through her telescope. She speaks to her monkeys, bidding them to do her dirty work so that she might finally possess the enchanted silver slippers that Dorothy is wearing.

Wicked Witch:

What is it, you flying pelt of fleas? (*Puts a telescope to her eye.*) Aha, I see them! That wretched Dorothy and her dog, and that Tin Woodsman, and Cowardly Lion, and that walking sack of straw. (*Lowers telescope.*) I know what I'll do. I'll destroy them with a pack of wolves. They have long legs and fierce eyes and sharp teeth. Or, I could send a great flock of wild crows, enough to darken the sky. They could peck them to pieces. Or, how about a swarm of black bees to sting them forever and ever! [...]

Capture the Lion, bring him to me. I'll harness him like a horse and make him work. Destroy the Scarecrow and the Tin

Woodsman and seize Dorothy. I must have those silver slippers. Quickly, hide yourselves so they do not see you. *(Winged Monkeys exit.)*

(Using the telescope again, gradually moves it to suggest Dorothy and her friends are approaching.) Good, good. They're coming right this way. Closer, closer. Almost here... Welcome "friends," to the domain of the Wicked Witch of the West. *(Cackles.)* Remember, Dorothy, your good friend, Glinda the Good, has no power here.

Yearbook

By Steven Fendrich

About the play: Four high school students are sneaking a peak at this year's yearbook. As they scroll through the pages and comment on the pictures, flashback scenes come to life onstage, telling the story behind each image. Through these vignettes, the students come to have a better understanding of one another, realizing that none of them fits neatly into any of the high school stereotypes with which they are so often associated.

Time period: The present.

Cathy
16 - 18

About the scene: Cathy is a yearbook photographer who has just been assigned the dreaded task of taking pictures of "Jock Block," the hallway where the most popular jocks and cheerleaders gather. Cathy is definitely not part of this clique and is scared to go there alone. In fact, she is so anxious she has a nightmare about it. In this monologue, Cathy relives her nightmare to two friends.

Cathy:

You know what they say about Jock Block? Well, all I know is that I had a dream. Call it a nightmare. *(Fearful.)* It was a gloomy, stormy day. I was sitting alone in this very hallway facing Jock Block. *(Pointedly to Susan and Marsha.)* As I stood in rightful fear, the two of you unmercifully ordered me to venture into a world of horror. I had to go. How else would I get my yearbook? So I crept slowly. *(Crosses very slowly. Shudders.)*

I'll never forget those sweat-filled cobwebs in the rusty open lockers. There was even a shower head in one, slowly dripping water in its shallow domain! How come some people never turn off the faucet all the way? *(Raises feet.)* Anyway, the floor was sticky from Gatorade, the containers scattered around the hallway. Broken baseball bats rose out of the ground like dead trees! The creaking sounds of petrified pom poms gave me goosebumps. Hideous haunting sounds oozed from the woodwork.

Whoever or wherever you evil jocks are, come out and face an innocent yearbook photographer. I have been brutally ordered by my yearbook editor to take pictures of you animals. If I don't return with pictures, I will be denied my yearbook. *(Cries.)* All I want is a few pictures of you guys so I can get my yearbook! *(As if somebody has grasped her arm.)* Oh, help! Help! *(Snaps out of the dream. Back to Susan and Marsha.)* So, do you understand now why I can't go down that hallway alone?

Appendix A
Monologues by Tone
♦♦♦
Comedic Monologues (C)

Play	Character	Age	Year
An Act of Piracy	Vivian	30s-40s	17th century
Anne of Green Gables	Anne [2]	Early teens	1870s
Bad Dates	Katy	20s	Present
Bedlam and Breakfast	Millie	Teens	1959
Camp Stowaways	Major Marjorie	30s-50s	Present
The Canterbury Tales	Wife of Bath	40s - 50s	1300s
Diary of Adam and Eve	Eve	Young adult	Beginning of time
Disorder in the Court	Glen	20s-30s	Present
Grover	Wife	20s-early 30s	Present
High-Rise High Jinks	Dawn	Early 20s	Present
In the Hood	Miss Bowman	50s-60s	Present
Life Is Like a Double Cheeseburger	Amy	20s	Present
	Liz	27 years old	
Love at First Thought	Jolaine	Late teens-early 20s	Present
The Most Viewed Least Watched Talk Show in History	Quinn	20s	Present
Rememberin' Stuff	Josephine	Teens	Present
The Secret Garden	Martha	20s or older	1911
Shakespeare by Monkeys	Riley	20s-30s	Present
Sir Huey and the Dragon	Dragon	Ageless	Once upon a time
Snow White Variety Show, The	Evil Queen	40s-50s	Once upon a time

Comedic monologues cont.

Play	Character	Age	Year
Stuck	Melissa	13-16	2020
The Wonderful Wizard of Oz	Wicked Witch	Ageless	Once upon a time
Yearbook	Cathy	16-18	Present

Seriocomic Monologues (S)

Play	Character	Age	Year
Anne of Green Gables	Marilla	50s	1870s
	Anne [1]	11 years old	
Beautiful	Gabrielle	Late-teens-20s	Present
The Gift	Ivy	Late teens-early 20s	Present
If These Walls Could Talk	Gloria	Teens	Present
	Rose-Marie		
	Teen Elaine		
Life Is Like a Double Cheeseburger	Carla	40s	Present
Little Women	Jo	Late teens-early 20s	1860s
The Ninth Train	Analise	18 years old	1939
Playground	Margaret	10 years old	Present
Pride and Prejudice	Elizabeth	20s	Early 1800s
Stopping at Ellis Island	Katie	20s	1906
The Virtual Family	Daughter	Teens	2020
Womanspeak	Sojourner Truth	53 years old	1850

Dramatic Monologues (D)

Play	Character	Age	Year
Admissions	Evelyn	50s	Present
Alive	Ashley	20s-30s	Present
Always Bella	Bella	Teens	Present
The Amazing Majesto	Blaire	40s-50s	Present
Amelia, Once More	Shelly [1]	20s-30s	Present
	Laura	Late 20s - early 30s	
	Shelly [2]	20s-30s	
Big Boys Don't Cry	Ms. Roberts	30s-40s	Present
	Ethel	32 years old	
A Bowl of Soup	Milly	16-18	Present
The Boy with No Name	Kathy [1]	Mid - late 30s	1980s
	Kathy [2]		
But I'm Only Seventeen	Mary	17 years old	Present
	She		
Cirrius, Nebraska	Rose	20s	Present
Door to Door	Trish [combined]	5 years old, late 40s, mid 60s	Present
Dracula	Mina	Mid 20s - mid 30s	1890s
The Empty Chair	Speaker #5	Teens	Present
Fighting for My Self	Juanita	Teens	1990s
	Kim	18 years old	
	Liz	Teens	
	Marcy		
Fosters	Anna	Teens	Present
Hush	Katie	19 years old	Present
Julian	Julian	60s	Early 1400s
A Lass Unparalleled	Lola [1]	58 years old	1960s
	Lola [2]		

Dramatic monologues cont.

Play	Character	Age	Year
The Last Leaf	Sue	20s	1907
Little Women	Amy	Teens	1860s
Mayfair Lady	Eliza	20s	1912
Memory Garden	Angie [1]	35 years old	Present
	Angie [2]		
The Mirror of Dori Gray	Dori	16-18	Present
	Samantha	Mid - late 30s	
The Ninth Train	Edna	30s-40s	1939
	Ruza		
Nobody Heard Me Cry	Mary	40s	Present
Pandora's Backpack	Liz	16-18	Present
Pollyanna	Mrs. Payson	Late 40s-50s	1910
Pride and Prejudice	Lydia	Late teens-early 20s	Early 1800s
Purple Ink	Kay	40s	Present
	Carol	60s	
	Melody	Late 30s-early 40s	
Quaran-Teens	Morgan	Teens	2020
Rememberin' Stuff	Barbara	Teens	Present
	Melissa Anne		
Salem's Daughter	Sarah Brooks	Early 20s-40s	1692
	Heather	18 years old	Present
Staying Home	Lisa	18-19	Present
Stuck	Unnamed	Teens	2020
Tested	Abigail	Teens	Present
Thistle Blossoms	Lisa	18-22	Present
	Jo	30s-60s	
The Turret Rose	Adeline	30s-40s	1970s
	Catherine	12 years old	
The Waiting Room	Granddaughter	20s-30s	Present

Play	Character	Age	Year
Walkin' Home	Nora	22 years old	Present
	Sonja	19 years old	
	Jenny	40s	
War Letters	Karen	Mid 30s	1990s
	Mary [1]	13 years old	
	Mary [2]		
Whispers	Kate	Teens	2018
Why Darkness Seems So Light	Mrs. Appleton	40s-50s	Present

Appendix B
Monologues by Time Period

Year	Play	Character	Age	Tone
Once upon a time	*Sir Huey and the Dragon*	Dragon	Ageless	C
	The Snow White Variety Show	Evil Queen	40s-50s	C
	The Wonderful Wizard of Oz	Wicked Witch	Ageless	C
Beginning of time	*Diary of Adam and Eve*	Eve	Young adult	C
1300s	*The Canterbury Tales*	Wife of Bath	40s - 50s	C
Early 1400s	*Julian*	Julian	60s	D
1692	*Salem's Daughter*	Sarah Brooks	Early 20s-40s	D
17th century	*An Act of Piracy*	Vivian	30s-40s	C
Early 1800s	*Pride and Prejudice*	Elizabeth	20s	S
		Lydia	Late teens-early 20s	D
1850	*Womanspeak*	Sojourner Truth	53 years old	S
1860s	*Little Women*	Amy	Teens	D
		Jo	Late teens -early 20s	S
1870s	*Anne of Green Gables*	Marilla	50s	S
		Anne [1]	11 years old	
		Anne [2]	Early teens	C
1890s	*Dracula*	Mina	Mid 20s - mid 30s	D
1906	*Stopping at Ellis Island*	Katie	20s	S
1907	*The Last Leaf*	Sue	20s	D

Year	Play	Character	Age	Tone
1910	*Pollyanna*	Mrs. Payson	Late 40s - 50s	D
1911	*The Secret Garden*	Martha	20s or older	C
1912	*Mayfair Lady*	Eliza	20s	D
1939	*The Ninth Train*	Analise	18 years old	S
		Edna	30s-40s	D
		Ruza		
1959	*Bedlam and Breakfast*	Millie	Teens	C
1960s	*A Lass Unparalleled*	Lola [1]	58 years old	D
		Lola [2]		
1970s	*The Turret Rose*	Adeline	30s-40s	D
		Catherine	12 years old	
1980s	*The Boy with No Name*	Kathy [1]	Mid - late 30s	D
		Kathy [2]		
1990s	*Fighting for My Self*	Juanita	Teens	D
		Kim	18 years old	
		Liz	Teens	
		Marcy		
	War Letters	Karen	Mid 30s	D
		Mary [1]	13 years old	
		Mary [2]		
2018	*Whispers*	Kate	Teens	D
2020	*Quaran-Teens*	Morgan	Teens	D
	The Virtual Family	Daughter	Teens	S
	Stuck	Melissa	13-16	C
		Unnamed	Teens	D
Present	*Admissions*	Evelyn	50s	D
	Alive	Ashley	20s-30s	D
	Always Bella	Bella	Teens	D
	The Amazing Majesto	Blaire	40s-50s	D

Monologues by time period cont.

Year	Play	Character	Age	Tone
Present	*Amelia, Once More*	Shelly [1]	20s-30s	D
		Shelly [2]		
		Laura	Late 20s-early 30s	
	Bad Dates	Katy	20s	C
	Beautiful	Gabrielle	Late teens - 20s	S
	Big Boys Don't Cry	Ms. Roberts	30s-40s	D
		Ethel	32 years old	
	A Bowl of Soup	Milly	16-18	D
	But I'm Only Seventeen	Mary	17 years old	D
		She		
	Camp Stowaways	Major Marjorie	30s-50s	C
	Cirrius, Nebraska	Rose	20s	D
	Disorder in the Court	Glen	20s-30s	C
	Door to Door	Trish [combined]	5 years old, late 40s, mid 60s	D
	The Empty Chair	Speaker #5	Teens	D
	Fosters	Anna	Teens	D
	The Gift	Ivy	Late teens - early 20s	S
	Grover	Wife	20s-early 30s	C
	High-Rise High Jinks	Dawn	Early 20s	C
	Hush	Katie	19 years old	D
	If These Walls Could Talk	Gloria	Teens	S
		Rose-Marie		
		Teen Elaine		

Year	Play	Character	Age	Tone
Present	*In the Hood*	Miss Bowman	50s-60s	C
	Life Is Like a Double Cheeseburger	Amy	20s	C
		Carla	40s	S
		Liz	27 years old	C
	Love at First Thought	Jolaine	Late teens - early 20s	C
	Memory Garden	Angie [1]	35 years old	D
		Angie [2]		
	The Mirror of Dori Gray	Dori	16-18	D
		Samantha	Mid - late 30s	
	The Most Viewed Least Watched Talk Show in History	Quinn	20s	C
	Nobody Heard Me Cry	Mary	40s	D
	Pandora's Backpack	Liz	16-18	D
	Playground	Margaret	10 years old	S
	Purple Ink	Kay	40s	D
		Carol	60s	
		Melody	Late 30s- early 40s	
	Rememberin' Stuff	Barbara	Teens	D
		Josephine		C
		Melissa Anne		D
	Salem's Daughter	Heather	18 years old	D
	Shakespeare by Monkeys	Riley	20s-30s	C
	Staying Home	Lisa	18-19	D
	Tested	Abigail	Teens	D

Monologues by time period cont.

Year	Play	Character	Age	Tone
Present	*Thistle Blossoms*	Lisa	18-22	D
		Jo	30s-60s	
	The Waiting Room	Granddaughter	20s-30s	D
	Walkin' Home	Jenny	40s	D
		Nora	22 years old	
		Sonja	19 years old	
	Why Darkness Seems So Light	Mrs. Appleton	40s-50s	D
	Yearbook	Cathy	16-18	C

Appendix C
Monologues by Character Age
◆◆◆

Age	Play	Character	Year	Tone
5 years old, late 40s, mid 60s	*Door to Door* [combined]	Trish	Present	D
Young adult	*Diary of Adam and Eve*	Eve	Beginning of time	C
10 years old	*Playground*	Margaret	Present	S
11 years old	*Anne of Green Gables*	Anne [1]	1870s	S
Early teens		Anne [2]		C
12 years old	*The Turret Rose*	Catherine	1970s	D
13 years old	*War Letters*	Mary [1]	1990s	D
		Mary [2]		
Teens	*Always Bella*	Bella	Present	D
	Bedlam and Breakfast	Millie	1959	C
	The Empty Chair	Speaker #5	Present	D
	Fighting for My Self	Juanita	1990s	D
		Liz		
		Marcy		
	Fosters	Anna	Present	D
	If These Walls Could Talk	Gloria	Present	S
		Rose-Marie		
		Teen Elaine		
	Little Women	Amy	1860s	D
	Quaran-Teens	Morgan	2020	D
	Rememberin' Stuff	Barbara	Present	D
		Josephine		C
		Melissa Anne		D

Monologues by character age cont.

Age	Play	Character	Year	Tone
Teens	*Stuck*	Unnamed	2020	D
	Tested	Abigail	Present	D
	The Virtual Family	Daughter	2020	S
	Whispers	Kate	2018	D
13-16	*Stuck*	Melissa	2020	C
Late-teens-20s	*Beautiful*	Gabrielle	Present	S
	The Gift	Ivy	Present	S
	Little Women	Jo	1860s	S
	Love at First Thought	Jolaine	Present	C
	Pride and Prejudice	Lydia	Early 1800s	D
16-18	*A Bowl of Soup*	Milly	Present	D
	The Mirror of Dori Gray	Dori	Present	D
	Pandora's Backpack	Liz	Present	D
	Yearbook	Cathy	Present	C
17 years old	*But I'm Only Seventeen*	Mary	Present	D
		She		
18 years old	*Fighting for My Self*	Kim	1990s	D
	The Ninth Train	Analise	1939	S
	Salem's Daughter	Heather	Present	D
18-19	*Staying Home*	Lisa	Present	D
18-22	*Thistle Blossoms*	Lisa	Present	D
19 years old	*Hush*	Katie	Present	D
	Walkin' Home	Sonja	Present	D
20s or older	*The Secret Garden*	Martha	1911	C
22 years old	*Walkin' Home*	Nora	Present	D
Early 20s	*High-Rise High Jinks*	Dawn	Present	C
Mid 20s - mid 30s	*Dracula*	Mina	1890s	D
27 years old	*Life Is Like a Double Cheeseburger*	Liz	Present	C

Age	Play	Character	Year	Tone
20s	*Bad Dates*	Katy	Present	C
	Cirrius, Nebraska	Rose	Present	D
	The Last Leaf	Sue	1907	D
	Life Is Like a Double Cheeseburger	Amy	Present	C
	Mayfair Lady	Eliza	1912	D
	The Most Viewed Least Watched Talk Show in History	Quinn	Present	C
	Pride and Prejudice	Elizabeth	Early 1800s	S
	Stopping at Ellis Island	Katie	1906	S
Early 20s-40s	*Salem's Daughter*	Sarah Brooks	1692	D
20s-early 30s	*Grover*	Wife	Present	C
20s-30s	*Alive*	Ashley	Present	D
	Amelia, Once More	Shelly [1]	Present	D
		Shelly [2]		
	Disorder in the Court	Glen	Present	C
	Shakespeare by Monkeys	Riley	Present	C
	The Waiting Room	Grandaughter	Present	D
Late 20s-early 30s	*Amelia, Once More*	Laura	Present	D
32 years old	*Big Boys Don't Cry*	Ethel	Present	D
35 years old	*Memory Garden*	Angie [1]	Present	D
		Angie [2]		
Mid - late 30s	*The Boy with No Name*	Kathy [1]	1980s	D
		Kathy [2]		
	The Mirror of Dori Gray	Samantha	Present	D
Mid 30s	*War Letters*	Karen	1990s	D
30s-40s	*An Act of Piracy*	Vivian	17th century	C
	Big Boys Don't Cry	Ms. Roberts	Present	D

Monologues by character age cont.

Age	Play	Character	Year	Tone
30s - 40s	*The Ninth Train*	Edna	1939	D
		Ruza		
	The Turret Rose	Adeline	1970s	D
Late 30s-early 40s	*Purple Ink*	Melody	Present	D
30s-50s	*Camp Stowaways*	Major Margorie	Present	C
30s-60s	*Thistle Blossoms*	Jo	Present	D
40s	*Life Is Like a Double Cheeseburger*	Carla	Present	S
	Nobody Heard Me Cry	Mary	Present	D
	Purple Ink	Kay	Present	D
	Walkin' Home	Jenny	Present	D
5 years old, <u>late 40s</u>, mid 60s	*Door to Door*-[combined]	Trish	Present	D
40s-50s	*The Amazing Majesto*	Blaire	Present	D
	The Canterbury Tales	Wife of Bath	1300s	C
	The Snow White Variety Show	Evil Queen	Once upon a time	C
	Why Darkness Seems So Light	Mrs. Appleton	Present	D
Late 40s-50s	*Pollyanna*	Mrs. Payson	1910	D
50s	*Admissions*	Evelyn	Present	D
	Anne of Green Gables	Marilla	1870s	S
50s-60s	*In the Hood*	Miss Bowman	Present	C
53 years old	*Womanspeak*	Sojourner Truth	1850	S
58 years old	*A Lass Unparalleled*	Lola [1]	1960s	D
		Lola [2]		

Age	Play	Character	Year	Tone
60s	*Julian*	Julian	Early 1400s	D
60s	*Purple Ink*	Carol	Present	D
5 years old, late 40s, <u>mid 60s</u>	*Door to Door*-[combined]	Trish	Present	D
Ageless	*Sir Huey and the Dragon*	Dragon	Once upon a time	C
	The Wonderful Wizard of Oz	Wicked Witch	Once upon a time	C